OCCASION[AL PAPER]

Aftermath of the CFA Franc Devaluation

by Jean A.P. Clément, with Johannes Mueller,
Stéphane Cossé, and Jean Le Dem

INTERNATIONAL MONETARY FUND
Washington DC
May 1996

Library of Congress Cataloging-in-Publication Data

Aftermath of the CFA franc devaluation / Jean A.P. Clément . . . [et al.].
p. cm. — (Occasional Paper ; 138)
Includes bibliographical references

ISBN 1-55775-561-2

1. French franc area. 2. Devaluation of Currency — Africa, French-speaking West. 3. Devaluation of Currency — Africa, French-speaking Equatorial. 4. Monetary policy — Africa, French-speaking West. 4. Monetary policy — Africa, French-speaking Equatorial. I. Clément, Jean A. P. II. Series: Occasional paper (International Monetary Fund) ; no.138.
HG3897.4.A34 1996 96-19859
332.4'966'0917541 — dc20 CIP

Price: US$15.00
(US$12.00 to full-time faculty members and
students at universities and colleges)

Please send orders to:
International Monetary Fund, Publication Services
700 19th Street, N.W., Washington, D.C. 20431, U.S.A.
Tel.: (202) 623-7430 Telefax: (202) 623-7201
Internet: publications@imf.org

recycled paper

Contents

Box

Tables

Section

Annex

Charts

Section

The following symbols have been used throughout this paper:

. . . to indicate that data are not available;

— to indicate that the figure is zero or less than half the final digit shown, or that the item does not exist;

– between years or months (e.g., 1991–92 or January–June) to indicate the years or months covered, including the beginning and ending years or months;

/ between years (e.g., 1991/92) to indicate a crop or fiscal (financial) year.

"Billion" means a thousand million.

Minor discrepancies between constituent figures and totals are due to rounding.

Preface

This Occasional Paper reviews developments in the countries of the CFA franc zone in the aftermath of the January 1994 CFA franc devaluation and discusses the challenges that lie ahead in securing a sustainable rate of growth in an environment of financial stability.

The paper draws largely on the report on "CFA Franc Countries—Recent Adjustment Experience and Policy Issues in the CFA Franc Countries" that was circulated for information to the Executive Board of the IMF in October 1995.

The authors are indebted to numerous colleagues throughout the IMF—particularly in the African Department—and the World Bank for comments on the paper. The authors wish especially to thank Evangelos A. Calamitsis and Christian Brachet for comments, guidance, and support. Thanks are also due to Paul Acquah, Anupam Basu, Pierre Dhonte, Christian François, Louis Goreux, Pierre Ewenczyk, Michel Galy, and Amor Tahari for insightful views, Ngoc Tuyêt Lê and Diep Nuven for research assistance, and Leslie Lefever for secretarial assistance. David Driscoll of the External Relations Department edited the paper for publication and coordinated production.

The opinions expressed in the paper are those of the authors and should not be construed as representing the views of the IMF or of its Executive Directors.

I Introduction and Background

Since its creation almost 50 years ago, the CFA franc zone has on balance served its members well.[1] The common currency, the CFA franc, has been freely convertible into French francs at a fixed rate and has provided an anchor for the economic and financial policies of the member countries. These countries benefited from a long period of remarkably low inflation and—until the mid-1980s—sustained economic growth. The discipline imposed on monetary policy by the arrangements of the zone ensured that appreciation of the currency exchange rate in real effective terms arising from inflationary financing was largely avoided.

After 1985, however, the economic and financial situation of the zone deteriorated as a consequence of two major shocks. First, the zone's terms of trade deteriorated by about 50 percent during the second half of the 1980s, owing mainly to a sharp drop in world market prices for its major export commodities, principally cocoa, coffee, cotton, and petroleum. Second, the external competitiveness of the zone weakened further as a result of the marked appreciation of the French franc against the currencies of the zone's other major trading partners. At the same time, the zone was increasingly handicapped by a number of structural and sectoral rigidities, particularly high unit-labor costs.

Despite repeated attempts at internal adjustment, especially to rein in wage costs and restructure the banking systems and public enterprises, per capita income fell steadily, and the economic and financial situation continued to worsen. With governments' wage expenditure claiming an increasing share of government revenues, and with transfers to public enterprises rising, the public sector financing requirements grew, crowding out the private sector. Very large domestic and external payments arrears were accumulated, aggravating the difficulties of the productive sectors and further weakening the banking systems. Under these circumstances, the zone's attractiveness to foreign investors diminished substantially—despite the advantage of stable prices and exchange rates—and capital flight increased appreciably.

These difficulties were reflected in a sharp deterioration of economic performance. Before 1985, economic growth in the CFA franc zone was generally much higher and more sustained than in the rest of Africa. Since 1986, however, output has remained virtually flat on average in the CFA franc zone, whereas it has expanded by an average of 2.8 percent a year in the other sub-Saharan African countries (Table 1). The contrast in terms of real per capita income changes is even starker. The overall fiscal and external current account deficits have been much larger in the CFA franc countries, and external debt has increased by more than 40 percentage points relative to GDP, compared with fewer than 30 percentage points on the average in other sub-Saharan African countries.

By the early 1990s, it had become increasingly clear that the adjustment strategy followed until then to address the deterioration in economic conditions in the 14 African member countries of the franc zone needed to be modified.[2] Indeed, given the size of the shocks that had buffeted the zone, reliance on measures of internal adjustment alone would have resulted in increased tax rates being imposed on a shrinking tax base and large cuts being effected in current and capital expenditure—particularly in education, health, and infrastructure—thereby jeopardizing the chances for a recovery of output growth.

In developing a more comprehensive adjustment strategy, the CFA franc countries strongly desired not only to preserve the existing regional monetary and exchange arrangements, including the nominal anchor, but also to strengthen monetary cooperation and deepen regional economic integration. The CFA franc countries recognized that a stable common currency rather than 13 separate national currencies increased the moneyness of their currency, reduced the

[1]See Box 1 for a profile of the CFA franc zone.

[2]While statistical information on the Comoros is provided in Annex I, this paper does not discuss the case of the Comoros, which is a member of the franc zone but not a member of a monetary union.

Box I. CFA Franc Zone: A Profile

The 14 African countries of the franc zone currently consist of two separate groups of sub-Saharan countries and the Islamic Federal Republic of the Comoros. The first group includes the seven members of the West African Economic and Monetary Union (WAEMU)—Benin, Burkina Faso, Côte d'Ivoire, Mali, Niger, Senegal, and Togo. The WAEMU was established on January 10, 1994, and supplemented the WAMU (West African Monetary Union), which has been in existence since November 14, 1973. The WAEMU treaty was ratified and became effective on August 1, 1994. The second group includes the six members of the Central African Economic and Monetary Union (CAEMC)—Cameroon, the Central African Republic (C.A.R.), Chad, the Congo, Equatorial Guinea, and Gabon. The CAEMC was established on March 16, 1994, together with two supporting conventions (CAMU—the Central African Monetary Union—and CAEU—the Central African Economic Union—as well as the CAECU—the Central African Economic and Customs Union). The CAEMC has not yet been ratified.

The two groups and the Comoros maintain separate currencies: the CFA franc, which stands for Communauté Financière Africaine in the WAEMU and for Coopération Financière en Afrique Centrale in the CAEMC; and the Comorian franc (CF) for the Comoros. The Banque Centrale des Etats de l'Afrique de l'Ouest (BCEAO) and the Banque des Etats de l'Afrique Centrale (BEAC) are the regional central banks of the WAEMU and CAEMC, respectively. As in the case of the Central Bank of the Comoros, each has an operations account with the French Treasury into which it deposits 65 percent of its foreign exchange holdings. Convertibility of their currencies into French francs through authorized intermediaries is supported by provision for central bank overdrafts on these accounts. The central banks are required by their statutes to maintain a 20 percent foreign exchange cover of their sight liabilities, a limit designed to act in practice as a barrier against open-ended access to the operations accounts that the banks maintain with the French Treasury.

Table 1. Economic and Financial Indicators for CFA Franc and Non–CFA Franc Sub-Saharan African Countries, 1975–93

	Average 1975–85	Average 1986–93
	(Annual percentage changes)	
Real GDP growth		
CFA	4.6	–0.2
Non–CFA	1.4	2.8
Real per capita GDP growth		
CFA	1.7	–3.1
Non–CFA	–1.3	–0.1
Inflation[1]		
CFA	11.8	1.0
Non–CFA	17.8	53.5
	(In percent of GDP)	
Overall fiscal balance		
CFA	–5.0	–7.2
Non–CFA	–6.1	–5.1
External current account balance (including grants)		
CFA	–6.5	–5.0
Non–CFA	–1.9	–0.9
External debt		
CFA	38.2	82.3
Non–CFA	25.2	53.9

Sources: Data provided by the authorities; and Fund staff estimates.

Note: Sub-Saharan Africa is defined here to include Nigeria and South Africa and to exclude Djibouti, Liberia, Mauritania, Somalia, and Sudan.

[1]Based on consumer price index.

risk element in holding it, and yielded information savings and facilitated transactions among members.

The pooling of official reserves also had a number of advantages. First, an adequate level of reserves held individually by each country would have required a higher level of aggregate reserves than if the union as a whole were to continue to pool reserves, given that the inter-country correlation between shocks is less than perfect. Second, intra-union payment imbalances, which are now automatically covered by internal credits, would become external imbalances that would need to be financed by the use of reserves. Third, there are economies of scale with spreading the overhead costs of transactions (via the merging of financial managements for reserves).

Finally, the common central banks—with their authority to safeguard the foreign exchange cover for currency issue and to administer statutory limits on individual governments' recourse to central bank credit—have had some measure of independence in determining credit policy, which would be difficult to emulate individually in each of the countries outside the framework of the existing monetary union. The monetary arrangements of the zone have had the advantage of preventing an excessive monetary financing of the fiscal deficits[3] and the related risk of

[3]The statutory ceiling on outstanding government borrowing from the common central banks is equivalent to 20 percent of recorded government revenue.

inflation, although this has entailed heavy government borrowing from abroad and bank borrowing by public enterprises and, in recent years, the accumulation of domestic and external payments arrears.

Thus, on January 11, 1994, the 14 African member countries of the franc zone decided collectively to broaden their adjustment strategy through a large change in the parity of their currencies, effective January 12, 1994, buttressed by a coherent set of macroeconomic and structural policies tailored to the circumstances of each country. The CFA franc countries also decided to strengthen their efforts toward economic integration.

The CFA franc was devalued by 50 percent in foreign currency terms, from CFAF 50 to CFAF 100 per French franc, and the Comorian franc was devalued by 33 percent, from CF 50 to CF 75 per French franc. The size of the parity change was determined on the basis of several indicators of the extent of the overvaluation of the CFA franc and the Comorian franc, including the evolution of the real effective exchange rate, the magnitude of the deterioration in the terms of trade since the mid-1980s, and the need to restore domestic and external equilibrium in the medium term.

This paper reviews developments in the CFA franc countries in the aftermath of the January 1994 CFA franc devaluation. After a brief summary of the new adjustment strategy (Section II), it describes the progress made and the difficulties encountered during 1994 and early 1995 in implementing the programs supported by use of Fund resources (Section III); and discusses the challenges that lie ahead in securing the conditions for the achievement of sustainable growth and financial viability over the medium term, taking into account the regional dimension of policies (Section IV). Preliminary conclusions are presented in Section V. There are five annexes to this paper: Annex I contains statistical information; Annex II provides a brief description of the ongoing regional integration efforts; Annex III reports on developments in monetary policy; Annex IV summarizes Fund technical assistance; and Annex V describes World Bank Group technical assistance.

II Modified Adjustment Strategy

Policy Framework

The realignment of the CFA franc parity in terms of the French franc in January 1994 represented a key modification of the adjustment strategy followed until then to address the rapidly deteriorating economic situation of the 14 member countries of the CFA franc zone. The devaluation was aimed at restoring macroeconomic viability in these countries, while preserving the monetary cohesion of the CFA franc zone and enhancing the momentum of economic integration. A key consideration in designing the new strategy was to ensure that the devaluation would be sufficiently large and supporting policies sufficiently strong to address the loss of competitiveness experienced during 1986–93 and thus give credibility to the new exchange rate.

The design of the individual country programs had to take into account the participation of member countries in the two regional economic and monetary arrangements—the WAEMU and the CAEMC—and the need to preserve the new peg of the CFA franc to the anchor currency, into which it remains freely convertible.[4] In such an environment, monetary policy can be formulated and implemented only at the regional level, geared to the defense of the parity, while national fiscal policies—including wage policy—aim at the restoration of domestic balance, and structural reforms seek to reduce market rigidities and remove impediments to growth.

With the fixed peg geared to holding down inflation, demand management policies have to be deployed to assure both internal and external balance. Therefore, the fundamental policy objective in the context of the medium-term programs of the CFA franc countries has been both to restore government savings and to generate such primary surpluses as would allow the stabilization/reduction (as the case might require) of the debt/GDP ratio, so as to increase public investment financed from domestic resources. As the domestic private sector over the past several years has been a negligible net saver in most countries and has been reluctant to hold claims on the public sector (which has translated into a lack of domestic or regional capital markets),[5] public debt in the CFA franc zone is mostly foreign held. At the same time, the statutory ceiling on central bank advances to the treasuries limits the room for monetizing fiscal deficits.[6] The restoration of fiscal viability is thus tantamount to the restoration of external viability, that is, the reduction of imbalances in the external current account to a level that can be financed spontaneously from abroad on a sustainable basis.

Attainment of macroeconomic viability so defined was predicated on a two-pronged strategy. First, government revenue was targeted to increase substantially through a broadening of the tax base, which was to more than compensate for a reduction of tax rates, especially on international trade. Second, government expenditure was to be curtailed, mainly through containment of the wage bill and subsidies to public enterprises. Higher government savings from these measures, combined with increased availability of foreign financing, were to allow for a recovery in public investment, the rapid elimination of external payments arrears, and the progressive reduction of domestic arrears. Sectoral allocations of government expenditure were to give priority to the development of human resources and essential infrastructure.

Fiscal objectives also had to be consistent with the ongoing efforts to harmonize and reduce external tariffs in the two subregions and with the attendant reduction in the relative contribution of international trade taxation to government revenue.[7] Policies had

[4]Given the weak foreign reserve position of the BCEAO and the BEAC at end-1993, the requirement to maintain a 20 percent foreign exchange cover of their sight liabilities imposed de facto a sizable reconstitution of the balances in the operation accounts in 1994 as an objective of policy.

[5]This can be traced largely to the earlier forced placement of government paper with bank and nonbank financial institutions and to the accumulation of arrears to the domestic private sector.

[6]The statutory ceiling on outstanding government borrowing from the common central banks was attained or exceeded by all countries during 1992–94.

[7]These measures have already resulted in the implementation of a common external tariff and a preferential internal tariff in the CAEMC. Progress in that direction is under way in the WAEMU.

to take into account the regional convergence criteria that were being developed in the WAEMU and, more recently, in the CAEMC, which are to serve as tools of regional surveillance.[8]

Structural reforms were designed to foster the conditions for sustainable growth over the medium term through the development of a competitive private sector and regional integration. The latter objective was seen, among other considerations, as a key to reducing the vulnerability of the zone to external shocks. Structural reforms centered on liberalizing domestic and international trade, including the virtual elimination of price controls and quantitative restrictions on imports, increasing flexibility in labor markets, streamlining government and reducing progressively its involvement in the productive sectors, and, where needed, restructuring the financial sector.

The medium-term macroeconomic frameworks were set out in the respective policy framework paper of all countries with programs supported by the Fund's structural adjustment facility/enhanced structural adjustment facility (SAF/ESAF).[9] In the other countries, the design of programs supported by stand-by arrangements from the Fund was also consistent with explicit medium-term frameworks. For a few stand-by arrangements, medium-term and structural policies were already elaborated in some detail (for example, for Cameroon and the Congo), and for all the programs, World Bank staff assisted the authorities in the design of policies in the Bank's area of expertise. The medium-term scenarios reflected the extremely difficult initial positions of most countries, characterized by negative growth, large fiscal and external imbalances, high debt/GDP and debt-service ratios, and sizable domestic and external payments arrears. The baseline paths of external current account adjustment took into consideration the strength of the policy package adopted, the need for reserve reconstitution at the subregional levels, and realistic assumptions about the potential access to normal inflows of foreign aid, including debt relief.

Medium-Term Objectives

To restore macroeconomic viability over the medium term, the programs adopted by the CFA franc countries generally aimed at achieving (1) an early stabilization of price increases, after the initial wave of corrective inflation attendant on the devaluation, at rates approximating those in the anchor country; (2) a resumption of investment and output growth based on a shift of resources to the tradable goods sector; (3) a rapid rebound in domestic savings and a significant narrowing of external current account imbalances; and (4) a strengthening of the two regional central banks' net foreign asset position.

Inflation was projected to accelerate sharply in early 1994 as a result of the pass-through of the devaluation and of modest increases in nominal wages; but it was to decelerate rapidly starting in the second half of the year. In the short run, inflation rates were expected to vary across countries. This was partly due to differences in country characteristics, such as the degree of openness, and in the likely changes in the terms of trade, but also because of the prospective differences in the pace of adjustment—including progress in reducing trade taxes, the scope and speed of price liberalization, and the extent of competition in domestic markets. Over the medium term, inflation rates were projected to decline and converge as a result of the common exchange rate anchor, the liberalization measures, and progress toward integration.

The new strategy sought to reverse the trend decline in *output*, with real GDP projected to grow on average by about 1 percent in 1994 and 4–6 percent on average over the medium term. The recovery of output was to derive from the shift in resources from low-growth protected sectors and nontraded goods activities to tradables in which countries enjoyed a comparative advantage. Agriculture, which employs most of the population, was expected to be the first to benefit from the exchange rate action because of higher producer prices for cash crops and the expected shift of domestic consumption toward domestic goods. Similarly, the sectors engaged in nontraditional exports and in the production of import substitutes were expected rapidly to utilize existing idle capacity, as well as to benefit from the cost compression efforts of previous years.

The average investment/GDP ratio was targeted to increase by about 4 percentage points to 19 percent in 1994 and by an additional 1–2 percentage points during 1995–96. At the same time, the strategy sought to narrow the *resource gap*—and ultimately the external current account deficit—by raising the domestic savings/GDP ratio by 5 percentage points to 18 percent in 1994 and by an additional 4 percentage points during 1995–96. The recovery in domestic savings was to derive from improvements in the public sector financial position, at the levels of both the Government and the public enterprises, and from improved profitability in the tradable goods sector. With the narrowing of the resource gap and an increase in official grants translating into smaller external current account deficits, a return of flight capital, and a higher level of external financial assistance, the net international reserve positions of the two regional central banks were expected to improve considerably in 1994 and remain strong thereafter.

[8]See Annex II.

[9]See Section II below for the status of arrangements with the Fund.

Fund-Supported Programs, Creditors, and Donors

Following the devaluation, 11 programs supported by use of Fund resources were put in place before end-March 1994, and the remaining two in May and September. In countries where the design of reforms and discussions on structural policy issues, including with the World Bank, were already at an advanced stage (Benin, Burkina Faso, Côte d'Ivoire, Equatorial Guinea, Mali, and Togo), programs could be supported forthwith by ESAF arrangements. In other countries (Cameroon, the Central African Republic (the C.A.R.), Chad, the Congo, Gabon, Niger, and Senegal), Fund support was extended initially through stand-by arrangements because speed was seen as of the essence to give a firm orientation to policies and medium-term strategies were not sufficiently articulated. In all of these cases, however, the expectation was that the stand-by arrangements would be replaced by arrangements under the ESAF or the extended Fund facility (EFF) as soon as conditions permitted and the initial programs had been implemented satisfactorily.[10]

All together, Fund financial support under the 13 arrangements (including multiyear arrangements) that were approved in 1994 amounted to about SDR 1.0 billion, for an overall average annual access of about 40 percent of quota (Annex I, Table 51). Program reviews were completed as scheduled with the WAEMU countries (except Niger) and with Gabon. In addition, the stand-by arrangement for Senegal was replaced by a three-year ESAF arrangement in August 1994.[11] With the exception of Gabon, the programs of the CAEMC countries went offtrack. Most of these countries, however, subsequently embarked on staff-monitored programs to re-establish the momentum of adjustment and pave the way for the eventual resumption of Fund financial support once policy performance had improved.

Fund and World Bank staff have cooperated closely in assisting these countries in the design of their adjustment programs, with the World Bank focusing on the structural, sectoral, social, and human resource aspects of policies. Bank disbursements of exceptional aid to the CFA franc countries in 1994 exceeded US$0.9 billion under Structural Adjustment Loans, Economic Recovery Credits, and other quick disbursing funds, as well as the Fifth Dimension (for Cameroon, Côte d'Ivoire, and Senegal). Furthermore, regional institutions, notably the African Development Bank and the European Union, as well as bilateral creditors, in particular, France, provided substantial exceptional financial assistance. The great majority of CFA franc countries also obtained rescheduling of eligible bilateral official debt and arrears under the auspices of the Paris Club in 1994, for an amount equivalent to about US$7 billion.

[10]Cameroon and the Congo became ESAF-eligible in February 1994 and May 1995, respectively. Gabon is not ESAF-eligible.

[11]The third annual arrangements under the ESAF for Benin, Burkina Faso, and Mali were approved on May 22, 1995, May 30, 1995, and April 11, 1995, respectively; and the second annual ESAF arrangement for Côte d'Ivoire was approved on May 19, 1995. The review under the first annual ESAF arrangement for Togo was completed on May 31, 1995, and the review under the first annual ESAF arrangement for Senegal was completed on June 9, 1995. Finally, an ESAF arrangement for Chad was approved on September 1, 1995, a new stand-by arrangement for Cameroon was approved on September 25, 1995, and an extended arrangement for Gabon was approved on November 8, 1995.

III Adjustment Experience

Overall Performance in 1994

On the whole, in 1994 the CFA franc countries broadly achieved—and at times exceeded—the objectives of their programs for economic growth, inflation, and improvement in the external position (Table 2 and Chart 1).[12] The process was helped by the recovery in world economic activity and the strengthening of non-oil primary commodity prices (particularly in the case of Cameroon and Côte d'Ivoire), as well as by ample rainfall in the Sahelian countries. Policies, however, played the principal role. In particular, with nominal wages kept firmly under control, inflation slowed down rapidly after the initial wave of price corrections, and output responded strongly to the gains in competitiveness. By contrast, performance was uneven on the fiscal and structural fronts. There were also important differences in performance between the member countries of the WAEMU and those of the CAEMC, in part because of unsettled political conditions in some of these countries or because of delays on the part of incoming governments in implementing needed measures.

In reviewing performance in the zone, the weaknesses in the statistical apparatus in most countries must be borne in mind. The quality, coverage, and availability of data on income, output and expenditure, prices, and employment and productivity are particularly weak. The coverage of fiscal operations also varies greatly. Improving the quality and timeliness of data is crucial to strengthening program design, implementation, and monitoring, and these improvements were indeed incorporated in a number of programs, often through performance criteria and benchmarks.

Inflation, as measured by the increase in the consumer price index (CPI), was brought under control throughout the zone after the initial surge in prices following the parity change.[13] Some further price corrections were necessary in several countries late in 1994 and in early 1995 as temporary price freezes on a few essential goods and public utilities were lifted or full pass-through was implemented. Progress in reducing inflation continued nonetheless (Annex I, Table 6, and Chart 2). Average annual inflation in 1994 was about 33 percent for the zone, with performance being somewhat better than targeted in the WAEMU and weaker in the CAEMC.[14] On a December-to-December basis, inflation ranged from 29 percent in Burkina Faso to 64 percent in the Congo. Twelve-month inflation continued to decelerate in most countries during the first half of 1995, to a range of 4 percent (Burkina Faso and Chad) to 16 percent (Benin).

With the reining in of inflation and the improvement in the terms of trade, *competitiveness* was strengthened. The depreciation of the CFA franc in real effective terms (measured in terms of relative CPIs) during 1994 is estimated at 30 percent for the zone: 32 percent for the WAEMU countries as a group and 26 percent for the CAEMC countries, broadly as expected in the programs (Annex I, Table 26, and Chart 3). If measured in terms of relative unit labor costs—which are difficult to document systematically but on which there is ample fragmentary information, for instance in Côte d'Ivoire and Cameroon—the real effective depreciation is estimated to have been significantly greater.[15] As a result, the improvement in competitiveness was particularly strong in sectors where the share of labor in total costs was relatively high and that of imported

[12]To facilitate comparisons, all data in this paper are shown on a calendar year basis. Accordingly, Cameroon's data, which are officially reported on a fiscal year (July–June) basis, have been converted for the purposes of this paper to a January–December basis.

[13]The CPI generally reflects urban consumption patterns, which are heavily tilted toward tradable goods; it thus tended to overestimate recorded inflation in the aftermath of the devaluation.

[14]An important factor in explaining the variations in inflation performance between countries appears to have been the degree of openness of the economy.

[15]Nominal wage increases were generally held in the range of 0–25 percent, a stance largely followed by the private sector. At the same time, because of the large unused capacity in late 1993, output growth (especially in manufacturing) did not translate into employment creation, suggesting large gains in productivity.

Table 2. Selected Economic and Financial Indicators, 1990–96

	WAEMU[1]						
			1994				
	1990–93 Average	1993	Original program	Provisional	Deviation	1995	1996
			(Annual percentage changes)				
Real sector							
Real rate of growth	0.3	–1.2	2.5	2.6	0.1	5.5	5.6
GDP deflator	–0.4	0.3	35.2	35.0	–0.2	8.7	3.2
Inflation (CPI)	0.5	0.5	31.9	29.7	–2.2	9.6	3.4
Nominal GDP	–0.2	–1.0	39.1	38.5	–0.6	14.8	9.0
			(In percent of GDP)				
Total consumption	90.6	92.5	86.4	86.0	–0.4	84.3	83.3
Total gross domestic investment	13.5	12.5	18.0	15.7	–2.3	16.7	18.0
Gross domestic savings	9.3	7.6	13.5	14.0	0.5	15.8	16.7
Resource balance	–4.1	–5.0	–4.4	–1.7	2.7	–1.0	–1.4
			(Annual percentage changes)				
Exports value (f.o.b.)[2]	–3.3	–3.6	120.8	109.3	–11.5	13.8	8.2
Exports (volume)[2]	–0.3	–3.5	4.4	4.7	0.3	7.3	8.5
Imports value (f.o.b.)[2]	–0.8	–4.7	105.5	75.6	–29.9	12.4	11.2
Imports (volume)[2]	–0.4	–5.8	–1.0	–9.9	–8.9	13.5	9.1
Terms of trade	–2.6	–2.8	–1.1	3.2	4.3	8.2	–1.9
Nominal effective exchange rates[2]	6.2	6.8	n.a.	–45.6	n.a.	n.a.	n.a.
Real effective exchange rates[2]	–2.1	–2.6	n.a.	–32.4	n.a.	n.a.	n.a.
			(In percent of GDP)				
Exports of goods and nonfactor serv.	25.3	24.2	37.4	35.1	–2.3	34.4	34.1
Imports of goods and nonfactor serv.	29.4	29.2	41.7	36.8	–4.9	35.4	35.4
External current account							
Excluding official transfers	–10.7	–10.8	–13.0	–8.0	5.0	–6.6	–6.7
Including official transfers	–5.8	–6.0	–6.8	–2.1	4.7	–2.8	–3.1
Total scheduled public debt serv.[3]	39.3	38.6	32.6	32.7	0.1	29.9	25.7
			(In percent of GDP)				
Fiscal							
Total government revenue[4]	17.3	15.4	16.6	15.9	–0.7	16.3	16.5
Total government tax revenue	14.1	12.8	14.1	13.2	–0.9	13.6	14.0
Domestic	9.9	9.1	8.0	8.2	0.2	8.2	8.7
International—exports	0.2	0.2	2.0	1.5	–0.5	1.6	1.4
—imports	4.1	3.6	4.1	3.6	–0.5	3.7	4.0
Total government expenditure	26.4	25.3	27.4	24.8	–2.6	23.4	22.3
Basic primary expenditure[5]	17.6	17.1	15.6	15.3	–0.3	14.2	13.4
Government wage bill	9.0	8.9	7.0	7.1	0.1	6.4	6.1
Government investment expenditure	4.9	4.7	7.1	5.9	–1.2	6.4	6.7
Public investment financed by internal resources	1.4	1.4	1.6	1.6	—	1.6	1.7
Basic primary balance[4]	–0.3	–1.6	1.0	0.6	–0.4	2.1	3.1
Overall fiscal balance[6]	–6.8	–7.5	–7.5	–5.7	1.8	–4.3	–3.6

inputs low (for example, agriculture, textiles, and light manufactures).

Economic growth in the zone is estimated at 1.3 percent in 1994, with strong momentum building up in the second half of the year and in early 1995. While this outcome was only slightly above original expectations, it represented an important reversal of past trends. Only two countries in the CAEMC, as expected, registered negative growth rates (Annex I, Table 4).[16] In most countries, output generally responded more rapidly than envisaged to the shift in relative prices. The structure of consumption also began to shift in favor of locally produced goods, such as food crops, vegetables, livestock, and light manufactures.

[16]The recovery of output, however, was pronounced in Cameroon beginning in the third quarter of 1994.

Table 2 ***(continued)***

	CAEMC[1]						
			1994				
	1990–93 Average	1993	Original program	Provisional	Deviation	1995	1996
			(Annual percentage changes)				
Real sector							
Real rate of growth	–1.2	–2.1	–1.1	–0.4	0.7	4.2	5.6
GDP deflator	–0.1	–1.3	33.9	38.4	4.5	7.7	3.2
Inflation (CPI)	–0.4	–1.7	33.3	37.3	4.0	10.2	3.6
Nominal GDP	–1.2	–3.6	32.9	38.0	5.1	12.3	8.8
			(In percent of GDP)				
Total consumption	80.3	80.7	75.1	70.1	–5.0	70.6	69.8
Total gross domestic investment	17.5	16.6	19.6	19.5	–0.1	20.8	21.9
Gross domestic savings	19.7	19.3	24.9	29.9	5.0	29.4	30.2
Resource balance	2.2	2.7	5.3	10.4	5.1	8.5	8.3
			(Annual percentage changes)				
Exports value (f.o.b.)[2]	–3.0	4.9	81.0	106.3	25.3	3.0	9.4
Exports (volume)[2]	0.2	1.9	1.0	5.8	4.8	1.3	7.1
Imports value (f.o.b.)[2]	–3.0	4.4	86.0	77.9	–8.1	9.5	10.0
Imports (volume)[2]	0.9	4.1	–7.2	–12.0	–4.8	11.2	6.7
Terms of trade	–0.1	3.0	–4.8	0.8	5.6	5.4	–3.6
Nominal effective exchange rates[2]	6.3	6.7	n.a.	–44.4	n.a.	n.a.	n.a.
Real effective exchange rates[2]	–4.3	–6.3	n.a.	–26.2	n.a.	n.a.	n.a.
			(In percent of GDP)				
Exports of goods and nonfactor serv.	30.1	30.8	41.2	45.4	4.2	41.5	41.2
Imports of goods and nonfactor serv.	28.2	28.2	33.6	36.0	2.4	33.3	33.6
External current account							
Excluding official transfers	–7.3	–7.5	–11.5	–4.1	7.4	–5.0	–4.6
Including official transfers	–4.4	–5.0	–7.9	–1.7	6.2	–2.7	–2.5
Total scheduled public debt serv.[3]	28.7	29.8	37.3	28.5	–8.8	37.9	31.3
			(In percent of GDP)				
Fiscal							
Total government revenue[4]	17.4	15.8	18.9	15.1	–3.8	17.8	18.6
Total government tax revenue	16.3	14.7	17.6	14.2	–3.4	17.0	17.4
Domestic	13.1	11.4	13.2	11.6	–1.6	13.4	13.6
International—exports	0.2	0.2	0.5	0.5	—	0.7	0.7
—imports	3.1	3.0	3.9	2.1	–1.8	2.7	2.9
Total government expenditure	26.4	26.1	28.5	22.7	–5.8	22.0	21.1
Basic primary expenditure[5]	17.8	18.1	14.6	12.5	–2.1	11.5	10.7
Government wage bill	9.6	9.8	7.3	6.5	–0.8	5.8	5.4
Government investment expenditure	5.1	4.9	6.5	3.9	–2.6	4.6	4.9
Public investment financed by internal resources	2.0	2.7	1.5	1.3	–0.2	1.3	1.3
Basic primary balance[4]	–0.5	–2.2	4.7	2.7	–2.0	6.3	7.7
Overall fiscal balance[6]	–7.9	–9.3	–6.6	–6.2	0.4	–2.7	–1.0

Production in the export-oriented agro-industrial and textile sectors rebounded, notably in enterprises that had been restructured or privatized in earlier years and were therefore well placed to benefit from the devaluation. Producer incentives were also restored by the increases in producer prices—ranging from 12 percent to 200 percent—for export crops (Annex I, Table 52). As a result, export volume in the zone increased by 5 percent in 1994, even though the crop season was already well advanced in certain countries at the time of the devaluation. Tourism also picked up, especially in Senegal. By contrast, production of nontradables, particularly construction and domestic services, has tended to remain depressed, except in Benin, Mali, Côte d'Ivoire, and Senegal. In general, enterprises in all sectors have continued to adapt, searching for new markets, financing, and suppliers.

Table 2 (*concluded*)

	CFA Zone[1]						
			1994				
	1990–93 Average	1993	Original program	Provisional	Deviation	1995	1996
			(Annual percentage changes)				
Real sector							
Real rate of growth	–0.4	–1.6	1.0	1.3	0.3	5.0	5.6
GDP deflator	–0.2	–0.4	34.7	36.5	1.8	8.3	3.2
Inflation (CPI)	0.1	–0.5	32.5	33.0	0.5	9.9	3.5
Nominal GDP	–0.7	–2.2	36.4	38.3	1.9	13.7	8.9
			(In percent of GDP)				
Total consumption	86.0	87.3	81.7	79.0	–2.7	78.3	77.4
Total gross domestic investment	15.3	14.3	18.7	17.4	–1.3	18.5	19.7
Gross domestic savings	14.0	12.8	18.3	21.0	2.7	21.7	22.6
Resource balance	–1.3	–1.6	–0.4	3.6	4.0	3.2	2.8
			(Annual percentage changes)				
Exports value (f.o.b.)[2]	–3.1	1.0	101.3	107.7	6.4	8.3	8.8
Exports (volume)[2]	–0.2	–1.1	3.0	5.2	2.2	4.7	7.9
Imports value (f.o.b.)[2]	–1.6	–1.2	98.6	76.5	–22.1	11.3	10.8
Imports (volume)[2]	0.2	–2.0	–3.2	–10.7	–7.5	12.6	8.2
Terms of trade	–1.5	–0.2	–2.6	2.1	4.8	7.0	–2.6
Nominal effective exchange rates[2]	6.3	6.7	n.a.	–45.1	n.a	n.a	n.a
Real effective exchange rates[2]	–3.1	–4.3	n.a.	–29.7	n.a	n.a	n.a
			(In percent of GDP)				
Exports of goods and nonfactor serv.	27.5	27.1	39.0	39.6	0.6	37.5	37.2
Imports of goods and nonfactor serv.	28.9	28.8	38.4	36.5	–1.9	34.5	34.6
External current account							
Excluding official transfers	–9.1	–9.1	–12.3	–6.3	6.0	–5.9	–5.8
Including official transfers	–5.2	–5.6	–7.3	–1.9	5.4	–2.8	–2.9
Total scheduled public debt serv.[3]	34.0	34.2	34.7	30.6	–4.1	33.8	28.4
			(In percent of GDP)				
Fiscal							
Total government revenue[4]	17.3	15.6	17.6	15.5	–2.1	17.0	17.4
Total government tax revenue	15.1	13.6	15.6	13.7	–1.9	15.0	15.5
Domestic	11.3	10.1	10.2	9.7	–0.5	10.5	10.9
International—exports	0.2	0.2	1.4	1.0	–0.4	1.2	1.1
—imports	3.6	3.3	4.0	2.9	–1.1	3.3	3.5
Total government expenditure	26.4	25.7	27.8	23.9	–3.9	22.8	21.8
Basic primary expenditure[5]	17.7	17.5	15.2	14.0	–1.2	13.0	12.2
Government wage bill	9.3	9.3	7.1	6.8	–0.3	6.1	5.8
Government investment expenditure	5.0	4.8	6.9	5.0	–1.9	5.6	5.9
Public investment financed by internal resources	1.7	1.9	1.5	1.5	—	1.5	1.6
Basic primary balance[4]	–0.4	–1.9	2.6	1.5	–1.1	4.0	5.1
Overall fiscal balance[6]	–7.3	–8.3	–7.1	–5.9	1.2	–3.6	–2.5

Sources: Data provided by the authorities; and Fund staff estimates and projections as of the end of May 1995.

[1]Weighted average using the corresponding GDP of the respective countries, except for exports and imports (value and volume).

[2]Three-year average (1991–93).

[3]In percent of exports of goods and nonfactor services.

[4]Excluding grants.

[5]Excluding interest payments due on domestic and foreign debt, foreign-financed investment, and net lending, but including domestically financed investment.

[6]Including grants.

Chart 1. Economic and Financial Indicators, 1990–96

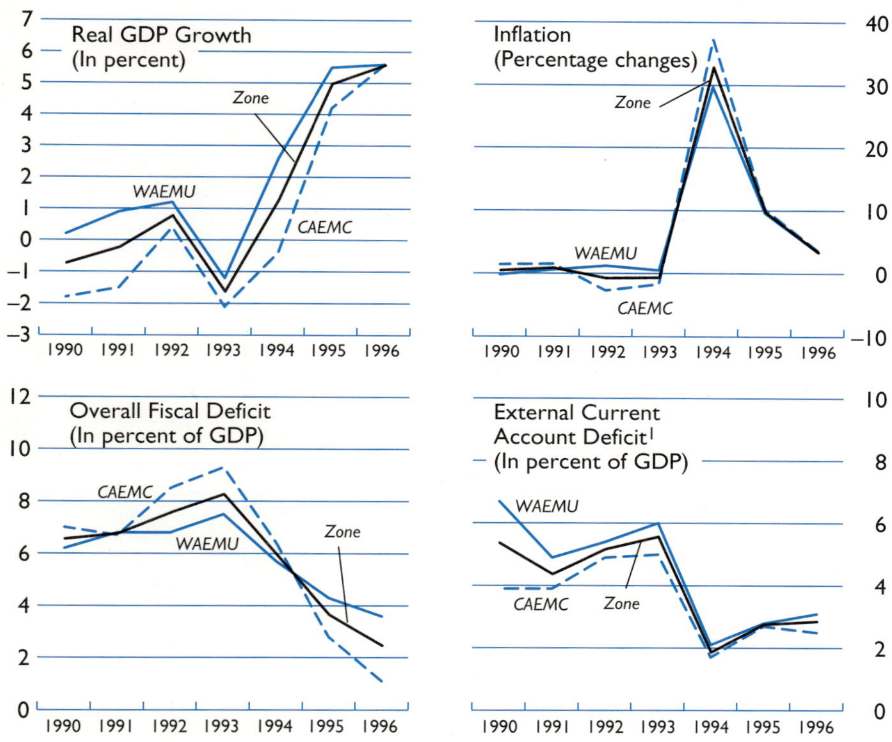

Sources: Data provided by the authorities; and Fund staff estimates as of the end of May 1995.
[1]Including grants.

With large income gains in the tradable goods sector, and falling domestic consumption, *gross domestic savings* in the zone increased by 8 percentage points of GDP, to 21 percent, in 1994 (Annex I, Table 12). The increase in the CAEMC (10 percentage points of GDP) was much higher relative to program than in the WAEMU (6 percentage points of GDP), and was concentrated in the private sector. By contrast, *gross domestic investment* rose by a mere 3 percentage points of GDP, to 17.5 percent, or somewhat less than intended (Annex I, Table 9).[17] Public investment was lower than programmed in all countries except Côte d'Ivoire, while private investment rose everywhere except in Benin and Senegal. The rise was particularly significant in the oil sector in the Congo, Equatorial Guinea, and Gabon. Private investment was also strong in the two largest economies, Cameroon and Côte d'Ivoire. However, private investment has remained confined to specific sectors, and has not yet picked up significantly in some countries. One reason that has been offered for this delay is the wait-and-see attitude of investors in the face of contracting domestic demand, a slow pace of repayment of government domestic payments arrears, and insufficiently forceful structural reforms.

Helped further by a substantial increase in foreign grants, the improvement in saving-investment balances translated into a major strengthening of *external current account positions* in most countries (Annex I, Tables 23 and 24). The improvement, which was concentrated in the trade balance, was better than envisaged in all cases except Equatorial

[17]For a full assessment of investment behavior one would have to take into account the import content of investment and the deflator of investment; however, detailed information is not yet available.

Chart 2. Quarterly Increases in Consumer Prices, 1994–March 1995

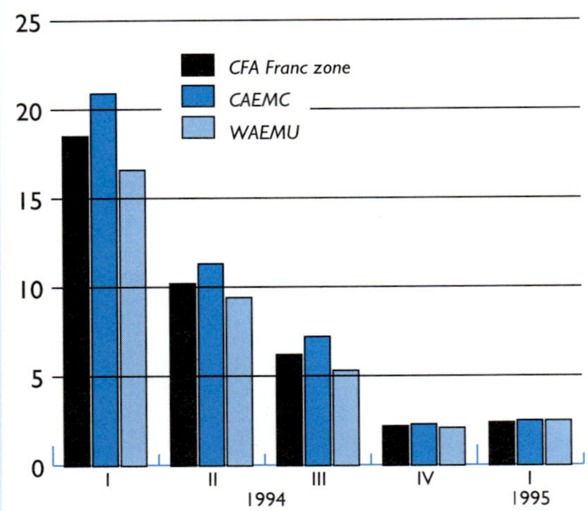

Sources: Data provided by the authorities; and Fund staff estimates.

Chart 3. Real Effective Exchange Rate and Terms of Trade, 1980–94

(Weighted by 1994 GDP; 1985=100)

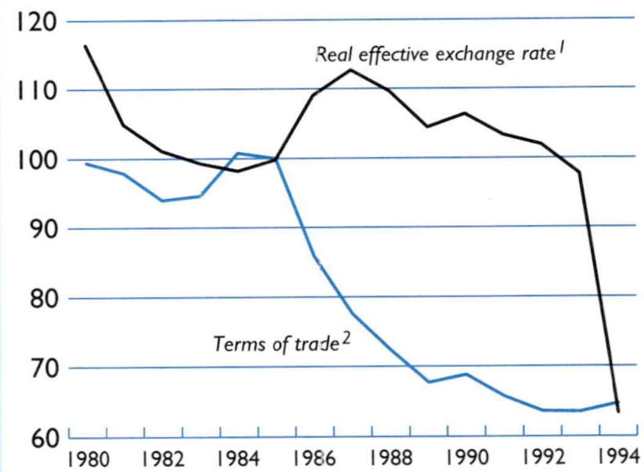

Sources: IMF, Information Notice System; *World Economic Outlook*; and Fund staff estimates.

[1]An upward movement of the real effective rate is an appreciation.

[2]A downward movement of the terms of trade is a loss.

Guinea, and was particularly strong in Côte d'Ivoire and Gabon. This was due largely to increases in export volume and to the sharp contraction in the quantity of imports, but also, especially in Côte d'Ivoire and Cameroon, to the strengthening of the terms of trade (Charts 4 and 5). Trade within the zone also appears to have increased rapidly—albeit from a low base—as zone products became more competitive vis-à-vis nonzone imports (Annex I, Table 22). In addition, trade flows with neighboring countries outside the zone (The Gambia, Ghana, and Nigeria) have been reversed, with a strong increase in exports (including re-exports from Benin and Togo) and a decline in imports.

The improvement in external current account positions, the resumption of foreign assistance, and large-scale repatriation of flight capital caused the *foreign reserve position* of the two common central banks to strengthen well beyond expectations. At end-1994, the BCEAO's position in its operations account with the French Treasury had improved by the equivalent of US$1.7 billion, and the BEAC's by US$0.3 billion. Gross reserves in months of imports of goods and nonfactor services increased to 1.8 months in the zone as a whole—2.4 months in the WAEMU and 1.0 month in the CAEMC.

All countries obtained comprehensive *debt relief* from the Paris Club in 1994 and early 1995, and most of them benefited from concessional terms. As noted above, total official debt relief amounted to about US$7.0 billion for 1994 (some US$200 million more than initially expected) (Annex I, Tables 28 and 50). The countries also benefited from substantial debt cancellation by a number of bilateral creditors, as well as large-scale exceptional assistance from bilateral and multilateral institutions (Annex I, Tables 47 and 48). However, there have also been delays in several cases in mobilizing aid disbursements, largely because of the nonobservance of applicable conditions, including those under Fund-supported and World Bank-supported programs.

Negotiated solutions to debts vis-à-vis commercial banks and other private creditors, which were virtually all in arrears at end-1993, were an integral part of the programs of Cameroon, the Congo, and Côte d'Ivoire. The authorities of these countries are continuing discussions with their private creditors with a view to developing solutions compatible with their external payments capacity and prospects.

In 1994 public external debt service due amounted to 31 percent of exports of goods and nonfactor services for the zone as a whole—33 percent in the WAEMU and 29 percent in the CAEMC. It approached 73 percent of government revenue in the WAEMU and exceeded 85 percent in the CAEMC

Chart 4. WAEMU: Decomposition of Trade Balance Variations, 1993–94
(In millions of U.S. dollars)

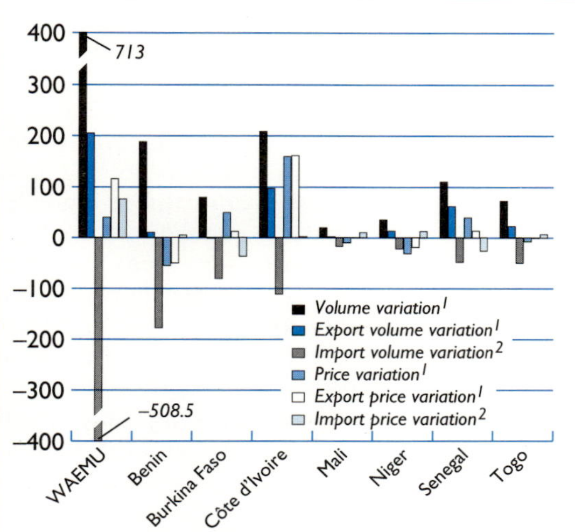

Sources: BCEAO; and Fund staff estimates.
[1]Positive numbers indicate improvements in the trade balance.
[2]Negative numbers indicate improvements in the trade balance.

Chart 5. CAEMC: Decomposition of Trade Balance Variations, 1993–94
(In millions of U.S. dollars)

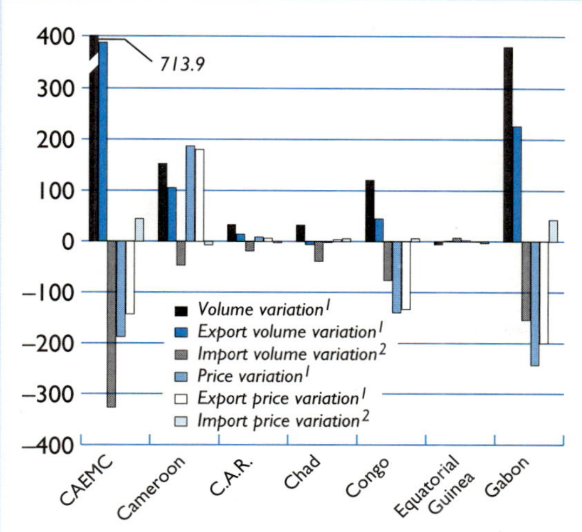

Sources: BEAC; and Fund staff estimates.
[1]Positive numbers indicate improvements in the trade balance.
[2]Negative numbers indicate improvements in the trade balance.

(Annex I, Tables 29 and 30). Public external debt outstanding at end-1994 represented 126 percent of GDP in the zone: 130 percent in the WAEMU and 122 percent in the CAEMC (Annex I, Table 27 and Chart 6). The average share of multilateral debt in total public external debt exceeded 30 percent for the zone, ranging from 15 percent in the case of Gabon to more than 80 percent in the case of Chad. Payments arrears on external debt service remained outstanding at end-1994 in all countries, except Benin, Mali, and Gabon. In the case of the Congo and Côte d'Ivoire, the bulk of these arrears were to foreign commercial banks.

Policies Supporting the Exchange Rate Adjustment

Wage and Labor Policies

In general, the authorities managed to keep a firm control over remuneration in the public sector, even against the backdrop of sizable nominal salary cuts in several countries in the course of 1993.[18] Nominal salary increases in the public sector were in line with targets in most countries—ranging from zero in Cameroon, Togo, and the Congo to 25 percent in Niger and Senegal, with most increases kept at 10-15 percent, as intended (Annex I, Table 39). The timing of these increases varied considerably across countries, including adjustments on account of past wage arrears (in Benin and Togo), wage drift, and family or other allowances. This wage restraint, combined with the liberalization of labor laws, in turn positively influenced wage formation in the private sector and in the state enterprises, where pay awards were in general only slightly higher than in the government sector. Developments in 1995 point to continued restraint in remuneration policy, with no general wage adjustments except in Côte d'Ivoire and Chad, where increases amounted to 5.5 percent and 10 percent, respectively.

Wage bills were also affected by reductions in government employment in most countries, except Burkina Faso, Niger, Togo, and Gabon. Overall, changes in government wage bills in 1994 ranged from minus 27 percent in Cameroon (following an 18 percent reduction the year before) to plus 28 percent in Togo, with a cluster of seven countries posting increases in the 10–15 percent range (Annex I, Table 38).

[18]Niger and Senegal in the WAEMU; and Chad (in late 1992), Cameroon, and the C.A.R. in the CAEMC.

Chart 6. External Public Debt at End of 1994
(In percent of GDP)

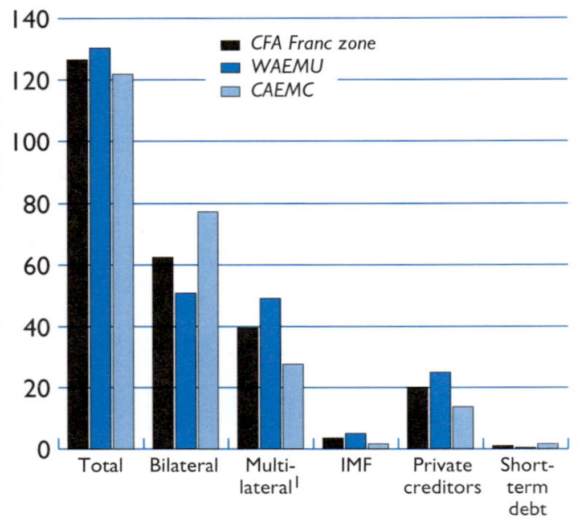

Sources: Data provided by the authorities; and Fund staff estimates.
[1]Excluding IMF.

At the same time, some progress was made toward liberalizing labor markets, particularly regulations applicable to hirings, firings, and minimum wages. Mali, Senegal, and Cameroon adopted new labor codes; the remaining countries are expected to do so in the next two to three years. With the continuation of a restrained wage policy, these reforms, including, in many cases, an alleviation of taxes on salaries and social security contributions paid by enterprises, should enhance the competitiveness of labor and help create jobs for a rapidly growing labor force (assuming that the tax burden is not shifted onto employees).[19]

Fiscal Developments and Policy

In 1994 there was a noticeable improvement in the "basic" primary government balance (that is, the current balance excluding interest and foreign grants, but including domestically financed investments) in all countries, except Burkina Faso and Niger, although the improvement was less than targeted in several cases (Annex I, Table 42).[20] The overall fiscal deficit relative to GDP also narrowed in more than half of the countries and, compared with the target, the overall deficit was lower in all countries except Cameroon, Chad, and the C.A.R. (Annex I, Table 43).

These overall results, however, were brought about through a fiscal policy mix that was often at variance with the programs. Contrary to original intentions, the brunt of fiscal adjustment tended, in most cases, to fall on current expenditure, including social spending, and, to a lesser extent, on investment outlays, as an offset to sizable shortfalls in tax revenue (particularly import-related revenue). Moreover, although foreign financing on the whole rose sharply, shortfalls in program assistance emerged in several countries. This, in turn, led to delays in the clearance of domestic and external payments arrears.

The weakest area of performance was *government revenue*. Tax and nontax collections fell substantially short of program in all CAEMC countries except Gabon, and in all WAEMU countries except Côte d'Ivoire, Mali, and Togo (Annex I, Table 31).[21] The ratio of total tax revenue to GDP reached only 13 percent in the WAEMU and 14 percent in the CAEMC in 1994, as against targets of 14 percent and 17.5 percent, respectively, mainly because import duty collections were well below programmed levels (Annex I, Tables 32–34). Consequently, the structure of government revenue shifted in 1994, with the share of domestic taxes rising at the expense of that of taxes on international trade (including export taxes), except in Côte d'Ivoire.[22]

While there are several reasons for the revenue shortfalls, both exogenous factors and policy slippages have been at play. There were strikes and civil unrest in some countries (for example, the C.A.R., Chad, the Congo, Equatorial Guinea, and Niger), as well as larger-than-expected reductions in overall domestic demand and shifts in the structure of consumption and imports toward less-taxed goods; the latter also reflected the expansion of intrazone trade.

[19]A recent study by France's Ministry of Cooperation shows that the wedge between wage costs and wage rates attributable to "fiscal and quasi-fiscal labor costs" represented up to one third of direct wage costs in 1993 (29 percent in Cameroon, 18 percent in Côte d'Ivoire, 32 percent in Mali, and 25 percent in Senegal).

[20]Because most public investment in the CFA franc zone is still governed by the availability of external financing, the basic primary balance criterion has served to measure fiscal adjustment on the basis of the variables that are under the control of the authorities.

[21]Compared with the established revenue targets, the largest shortfalls are estimated at 26 percent in the C.A.R., about 30 percent in Chad and Niger, and 40 percent in Cameroon.

[22]Several countries have low or no export taxes, while others have temporarily introduced or maintained such taxes (for example, Côte d'Ivoire in the WAEMU and most of the CAEMC countries).

Concerning policy implementation, revenue policies in general aimed to improve the tax structure and reduce reliance on trade taxation, while respecting the objectives for indirect tax harmonization in the region. In both subzones, harmonization and the reduction of indirect taxes and external tariffs took place as envisaged.[23] Following the devaluation, all countries reduced external tariffs considerably, including those on petroleum products. However, the impact of this reduction was not offset by the expected revenue impact of the expansion of the tax base and the strengthening of tax administration. The poor revenue performance highlighted the continuing problems afflicting tax administration, including weaknesses and fraud in customs, and the continued widespread granting of exemptions contrary to program undertakings, especially in the CAEMC countries, but in several countries in the WAEMU as well.[24] There were also difficulties in the early months of 1994 in implementing the tax reforms—particularly in the CAEMC—and, in many cases, in properly assessing the new tax base after the devaluation. The sharp decrease in the real wages of tax collectors and the related lack of incentives might also have been a factor behind the poor revenue performance.

Where revenue shortfalls developed, they were offset in most cases by deeper-than-envisaged cuts in *government expenditure*. Total expenditure fell by about one half of a percentage point of GDP in the WAEMU, but by 3.5 points in the CAEMC in 1994 (Annex I, Table 35). Primary expenditure was below program in all countries but Burkina Faso, the C.A.R., and Côte d'Ivoire (Annex I, Table 36). Since the wage bill was broadly on target in most countries—except Cameroon, where it was kept 1.5 percentage points of GDP below program, and Benin, the C.A.R., Niger, and the Congo, where it exceeded program objectives (Annex I, Tables 37 and 38)—the bulk of the economies made in current outlays was concentrated in nonwage expenditure, including social spending. Investment expenditure also remained below program in all countries, except Côte d'Ivoire. Scheduled interest payments, before rescheduling, were somewhat lower than programmed in all countries, except Togo. Overall, therefore, the composition of spending often deviated from program intentions.

In most cases, progress in improving budgetary procedures and expenditure control and information systems was limited. In several countries, the investment budget remained separate from the current budget, debt operations often continued to be left off budget (for example, in Côte d'Ivoire and Cameroon), and extrabudgetary operations persisted (for example, in Cameroon, Equatorial Guinea, and Gabon). While the practice of elaborating multiyear rolling public investment programs was generalized, little progress was made in developing techniques to appraise expenditure priorities. The coverage and quality of information on government financial operations also remained uneven.

In meeting their *financing* needs, all countries benefited in 1994 from extensive debt relief (two thirds of the total) and, except in the case of Equatorial Guinea, from a major increase in foreign assistance. In total, such financing more than tripled, to the equivalent of about US$11 billion or 30 percent of the zone's GDP, from the amounts obtainable a year earlier (Annex I, Table 47). In addition to Fund and World Bank assistance, considerable financial support was provided by France, the African Development Bank, and the European Union. There was nonetheless an overall shortfall in foreign financing of somewhat more than US$0.9 billion, mainly on account of shortfalls in exceptional budgetary assistance and project aid, although these were partly offset by higher debt relief. The shortfalls in most cases were traceable to the nonobservance of the applicable conditions, including under Fund arrangements.

The financing shortfalls contributed in turn to the nonobservance of certain program targets—mostly those related to the reduction and clearance of domestic payments arrears (Burkina Faso, the C.A.R., Chad, the Congo, and Niger)—as well as to external payments arrears (Côte d'Ivoire, Equatorial Guinea, Senegal, and Cameroon).

Monetary Developments and Policy

At the zone level, monetary developments in 1994 were dominated by a much faster reconstitution of real money balances than had been expected—a trend that pointed to the early return of confidence in the currency and to the credibility of the new exchange rate. *Broad money* increased about in line with nominal GDP, with velocity (year on year) remaining virtually unchanged in the WAEMU, and increasing only slightly in the CAEMC, the latter largely because of continued concerns over the

[23]In the CAEMC, the reduction was part of the customs tariff/indirect tax reform agreed in June 1993 in the framework of the CAECU. Details are provided in Annex II. No such comprehensive reform has been adopted yet by the WAEMU countries; nonetheless, since 1993, policies in these countries have been geared to reducing the level and dispersion of tariff rates and reducing or eliminating quantitative restrictions, thus fostering a measure of regional harmonization.

[24]The most pronounced deviations from program path were in Niger, Chad, the C.A.R., and particularly Cameroon. In this latter case, nominal GDP, imports, and exports all turned out higher in 1994 than envisaged in the program; yet, nominal tax collections declined in absolute terms compared with 1993, causing the tax/GDP ratio to fall from 11.5 percent in 1993 to 8.5 percent in 1994.

Chart 7. WAEMU: Monetary Survey, 1994
(Annual changes in percent of beginning-of-period money stock)

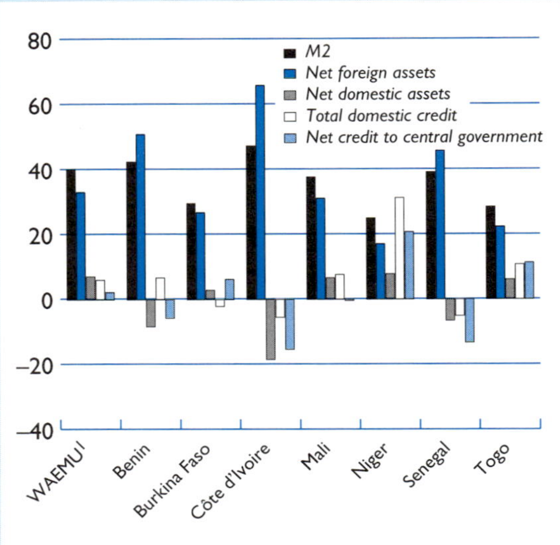

Sources: BCEAO; and Fund staff estimates.
[1]BCEAO definition.

Chart 8. CAEMC: Monetary Survey, 1994
(Annual changes in percent of beginning-of-period money stock)

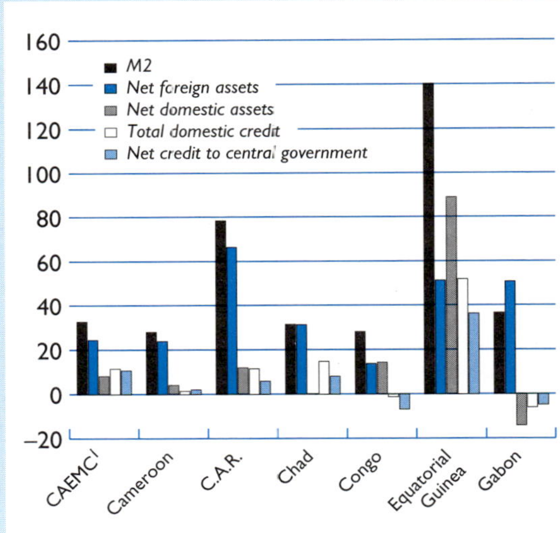

Sources: BEAC; and Fund staff estimates.
[1]BEAC definition.

health of some national banking systems. The increase in broad money was mostly in the form of currency in circulation, although the rate of growth varied from country to country. This was due partly to the fact that commercial banks discouraged private sector deposits in remunerated accounts because of lack of domestic use for their resources, and also to the absence of banking services in rural areas, which led farmers, who benefited from higher producer prices, to hold increasing amounts of cash.

In contrast to this rapid increase in bank liabilities to the private sector, *credit growth to the economy* in 1994 was sluggish in both subzones—amounting to 3.9 percent of beginning-of-period broad money in the WAEMU, and 0.8 percent in the CAEMC. In the tradable goods sector, internal fund generation appears to have been more than sufficient to meet financing needs, especially given the high international commodity prices. The repatriation of flight capital also helped dampen credit demand, as did the repayment of government domestic arrears. On the supply side, the high operational costs of commercial banks, the absence of active competition in the industry, the continued need for provisioning for doubtful loans, and the lack of collateral of most potential clients in the nontraded goods sectors all combined to foster great prudence in bank lending. At the same time, *net bank credit to governments* remained below ceilings in the majority of cases, reflecting the strengthening of public finances.[25]

In these conditions, the growth of the net domestic assets of the banking system in both subregions remained well below the increase in broad money, and thus *net foreign assets* improved substantially (Annex I, Tables 44 and 45). The recovery in the zone's combined net foreign asset position during 1994 was equivalent to US$2.2 billion—US$1.6 billion in the WAEMU and US$0.6 billion in the CAEMC, with the BEAC moving from a net debtor to a net creditor position.

In conducting monetary policy, the authorities relied principally on the discount rate and the intervention rate in their respective regional money markets; but these instruments were of limited effectiveness, given the surge in the liquidity of the banking systems throughout the zone as money balances were being reconstituted and credit demand remained sluggish (Annex I, Table 46, and Charts 7 and 8). In the immediate aftermath of the devaluation, the BCEAO and the BEAC raised their dis-

[25]In several countries, this helped bring outstanding recourse to central bank financing below the statutory ceiling for the first time in several years.

count rates[26] by 4 percentage points to 14.5 percent, and by 2.5 percentage points to 14.0 percent, respectively. These increases were followed by gradual downward adjustments as inflation abated, to 8.5 percent in the WAEMU in June 1995, and 8.0 percent in the CAEMC (auction rate) in December 1994 (before it returned to 8.75 percent in June 1995). The minimum rates on bank deposits fell from 8.0 percent in January 1994 to 4.5 percent in September 1994 in the WAEMU, and from 9.0 percent to 5.5 percent in the CAEMC. Maximum lending rates were lowered from 29.0 percent to 17.0 percent in the WAEMU, and from 19.0 percent to 16.0 percent in the CAEMC.

With the increase in their loanable resources, commercial banks drastically reduced their outstanding recourse to central bank financing, while raising their reserves with the monetary authorities in 1994 by 80 percent[27] and 278 percent, respectively, in the WAEMU and the CAEMC. In the WAEMU money market, offers greatly exceeded demand, and only a small portion of funds on offer was absorbed. To mop up the excess liquidity, the BCEAO decided to securitize the consolidated claims it held on the governments of the subregion on account of the restructuring of commercial banks during the late 1980s and early 1990s. These bonds have proved to be popular with banks, as they offer a way to place unremunerated reserves and improve the banks' financial health at, in practice, no opportunity cost.[28] However, as the banks can redeem the bonds at par at any time and use them to fulfill reserve requirements, any further attempt by the BCEAO to tighten monetary conditions will be less effective. Local commercial banks have also purchased bonds issued by other WAEMU countries. In Burkina Faso and Mali, most of the increase in the commercial banks' net foreign asset position was on account of the purchase of such claims on other WAEMU member governments.

In the CAEMC, flows in the regional interbank market tended to be largely directed to Gabon because of perceived bank risks elsewhere. In the money market, the BEAC injected reserves on a limited scale, mostly to support banks in difficulty in Cameroon and the Congo, which had no access to the regional interbank market.

[26]In the WAEMU, the discount rate is a de facto penalty rate that serves as a benchmark for the BCEAO's repurchase and auction rates. In the BEAC, the discount rate was replaced by the auction rate as the key intervention rate in July 1994.

[27]Including securitization as noted below.

[28]The bonds carry a tax-free, fixed interest rate of 5 percent for a 12-year maturity—compared with a yield of 5.5 percent in the money market—and are both quasi-liquid and risk free, as they are redeemable at par by the BCEAO on demand.

Structural Reforms

To strengthen the gains in competitiveness brought about by the devaluation and the tightening of domestic demand management, and to pave the way for a resumption of sustainable growth, structural reforms were launched or deepened in all countries with the support of the Fund, the World Bank, the European Union, and bilateral donors. The reforms focused mainly on public enterprises, the civil service, the legal and regulatory framework, and the trade regime. Overall, progress was significant, albeit generally slower than envisaged because of administrative weaknesses and of delays in adopting the necessary legislations.

Over the years, *public enterprises* have played a central role in the economies of the zone, but they have often acted as a deterrent to growth and a source of financial imbalances. The rehabilitation or privatization of these enterprises was therefore an integral part of most structural reform efforts envisaged under the programs. However, most countries fell short of their targets for divestiture and restructuring in 1994. Of a total of about 800 public enterprises, rehabilitation or liquidation procedures were initiated for only 50, or one half of the number originally targeted.

Public enterprise reform programs, though varying greatly from country to country, generally involved the privatization or restructuring of enterprises, breaking up monopolies and opening up activities to private sector competition, and improving the institutional and legal framework within which public enterprises operate, including providing the basis for greater management autonomy. In the cases where public enterprises were to remain in the government portfolio, restructuring measures typically involved the implementation of management enhancement systems, for example, through the introduction of modern cost accounting schemes, performance-based contracts, and improved financial monitoring mechanisms, price decontrols, cost recovery for state monopolies, efforts to cut costs, including reductions in staffing levels, and the clearance of arrears to the government and of cross-debts with other public enterprises.

The devaluation of the CFA franc facilitated the privatization of some public enterprises, particularly those involved in export, import substitution activities, and food processing, where extensive streamlining had already taken place before the exchange rate change. On the whole, however, most countries are still experiencing difficulties in selling off enterprises, as demand has not yet built up sufficiently for these assets. It may also be that the original speed of privatization itself was not suited to prevailing market conditions shortly after the devaluation. Thus, many countries are now revisiting elements of their divestiture strategy, for example, by assessing possible alternative terms of sale, management contracts, and ways to improve net asset valuation.

Civil service reform was another important component of structural reform programs. Consistent with the need to contain government wage bills, while making room for improvements over time in pay relativities, most countries have moved to freeze or reduce civil service employment. The main measures have included freezes on recruitment outside the priority areas of education and health, nonreplacement of retiring personnel, voluntary departure programs, and outright layoffs accompanied by severance pay in most cases. These actions have met with varying degrees of success. On the one hand, hiring freezes, nonreplacement of retiring employees, and reorganization or closing down of government units or public enterprises have generally proven successful in shedding excess personnel, albeit at a significant cost at times in terms of severance pay. On the other hand, voluntary departure programs in most countries have only produced a small decline in the number of civil servants, partly because of the inadequacy of available funds to promote such schemes on a large and attractive scale.

To promote private sector activities, most countries have embarked on a progressive overhauling of the *legal and regulatory framework* and have taken other steps to remove administrative hindrances to entrepreneurial initiative. The efforts form part of a regional strategy to harmonize key legislation on investment, business, insurance, social security, and labor relations. Accordingly, the programs provided for investment codes to be reformulated in practically all countries so as to make the legal and judicial environment more stable and predictable, while improving the incentives for foreign and domestic private investment. Most countries have also increased efforts to modernize corporate, commercial, and accounting laws. As part of this effort, nine members of the zone have already ratified the treaty establishing the Organization for the Harmonization of Business Law in Africa (OHADA), which seeks to adopt uniform regulations covering the main areas of business law, as well as to establish a regional court.[29]

In the area of *trade policy*, a simplified four-tier common external tariff (TEC) and a single intrazone tariff (currently at 20 percent of the TEC) have been largely in place in the CAEMC since early 1995 (except in Chad, which completed the process only in July 1995). Discussions on reductions in tariff levels and their dispersion, however, are still taking place in the WAEMU. In both subzones, quantitative restrictions have been largely dismantled and the rates of effective protection have been lowered and become less distortionary. There is some evidence that by lowering tax rates, these reforms helped lessen price pressures in the wake of the devaluation, as well as facilitate the rebound of the export sector. Meanwhile, all countries have endeavored to maintain an *exchange system* free of restrictions on payments and transfers for current international transactions.[30]

Social Policies

The partial or total pass-through of world market prices to producers in the cash crop sectors had a very salutory effect on the income of the rural populations, which had been affected the most by the growing distortions in relative prices during the period 1986–93. The corrective price changes, however, meant an erosion of purchasing power for the urban populations. For this reason, all programs incorporated policies to alleviate the transitional effects of adjustment on the most vulnerable groups and to improve the level and quality of social services, particularly in primary education and health.

One general approach followed by most countries was to reduce tax and tariff rates—or introduce temporary subsidies—on essential goods, in particular rice, sugar, flour, kerosene, and medicines. Another instrument that was used was recourse to selected and temporary price controls to prevent unrest and speculation, as well as possible snowballing expectations of an inflation spiral. Administered prices typically covered petroleum products (ten countries), water (nine), electricity (nine), bread (nine), rice (nine), edible oil (eight), and sugar (seven). With inflationary pressures abating as the year advanced, however, most of these controls have been removed and prices adjusted, except in a few cases where the pace of liberalization is governed by understandings reached under external support operations.

Many programs have also included targeted social safety nets. These initiatives have typically consisted of budgetary allocations for labor-intensive public works aimed at creating employment in urban areas (for example, in Burkina Faso, Cameroon, and Côte d'Ivoire); vocational training programs for youth; and promotion of small businesses as, for instance, in Benin and Cameroon. However, implementation has often been hampered by lack of appropriate instruments, insufficient preparation, and limited administrative capacity, which in turn have caused international support to lag.

[29]See Annex II.

[30]There are national limits on foreign exchange allowances for travel, study, and medical care abroad in a number of countries, but these are normative and all bona fide transactions are allowed.

On a broader level, all programs have sought, with the assistance of the World Bank and bilateral donors, to place emphasis on human resource development, particularly in primary education and health. Although expenditure on social programs increased in real terms in some countries in 1994, in general, progress toward the reallocation of spending remained modest because of the shortfalls in domestic revenue collections. This reallocation therefore continues to be a central feature of the programs formulated for 1995 and beyond.

IV Challenges Ahead

The short-term objectives of the programs adopted in support of the devaluation were broadly met in 1994 and the first part of 1995, but a return to sustained growth and external viability will require substantial progress in the areas of fiscal adjustment and structural reform. Thus, the challenges facing the CFA franc countries in the period ahead are how to translate these early encouraging results into long-term gains.

In about half the countries of the zone, there is a need to continue fiscal consolidation and to deepen the structural reforms undertaken since early 1994. In the other half, there is a need to reposition economies on a path of reform and to correct the policy slippages that occurred in 1994. In a few countries, this effort at adjusting course has been under way in the framework of staff-monitored programs since the middle or the end of 1994, and it is crucial that the remaining countries follow suit without delay.

To achieve these objectives, the strategy adopted in the wake of the devaluation remains broadly appropriate. It is particularly important that demand management policies are consistent with the new level of the exchange rate anchor—that is, with very low inflation—and that supply-side actions are conducive to a generation and allocation of resources that will place the countries of the zone on a sustainable growth path.

Monetary policy under the fixed peg regime should continue to center on preserving the credibility of the exchange rate, and therefore on maintaining an adequate level of foreign assets in the two regional central banks. The liberalization and eventual integration of subregional financial markets are increasingly reducing the relevance of monetary and credit aggregates and policies at the national level, creating new operational challenges for the design and monitoring of individual country programs. These developments thus call for the strengthening of policy formulation and implementation at the regional central bank level.

Fiscal policy remains the central tool of domestic adjustment. First, fiscal policy forcefully affects cost behavior in the nontraded goods sector, inter alia, through government wage policies. Second, there is a need to bolster domestic savings both to support the recovery of investment and to keep the external current account positions on a trend consistent with the reestablishment of external viability (as defined earlier); and increasing public sector savings makes the most direct and predictable contribution to domestic resource mobilization. Fiscal consolidation, in turn, should facilitate the early regularization of payments arrears to the domestic private sector. Third, given the continued heavy debt-service burden and the weight of payments arrears, establishing fiscal sustainability and policy credibility calls for the generation of sizable primary surpluses that stabilize and, where needed, reduce public debt/GDP ratios. This effort needs to be complemented by similar improvements in the financial position of the nongovernmental public sector to lessen overall public sector pressures on resources and allow the private sector to serve as the engine of growth. Fourth, the resumption of orderly relations between member countries' governments and their creditors will help restore creditworthiness and eventually facilitate the mobilization of foreign private saving to finance domestic investment.

Complementary *structural reforms*, at both the national and the regional levels, need to be accelerated to create an environment that fosters private initiative, unlocks the potential for economic diversification, and thus raises the rate of growth of potential output. In particular, the removal of impediments to intrazone goods and factor mobility should buttress the countries' resilience to external shocks.

Fiscal Policy

As noted earlier, progress has been made in reducing fiscal imbalances in the zone since the devaluation, but the adjustment has lagged in three respects. First, in several countries the overall improvement in (current) primary balances fell short of program targets in 1994; moreover, additional adjustment over time was originally envisaged as foreign assistance was expected to taper off or decline. Second, there is a need to change the structure of public finances, as the large shortfalls in revenue caused the brunt of adjustment to fall disproportionately on nonwage current and investment expenditure, thus weakening the basis for long-term growth. Finally, several countries need to eliminate domestic payments arrears.

More specifically, to achieve a more sustainable fiscal position, CFA franc countries as a group should increase their primary surplus at least by 3.5 percentage points of GDP to 5 percent of GDP on average in 1996. To this end, these countries will need to adopt new revenue measures, including reforms centered on broadening the tax base and addressing administrative deficiencies, as well as continue to contain public spending. In addition, outlays will need to be allocated according to stricter economic and social criteria, and to be reoriented toward human capital and infrastructure, a process that is expected to be helped by the public expenditure reviews carried out with the assistance of the World Bank.

Improving Government Revenue Performance

The government revenue experience in 1994 indicates the need to strengthen four main areas. First, the ratio of tax collections to GDP—except in Côte d'Ivoire, the Congo, and Gabon—has been relatively low, ranging from 5 percent to 13 percent. Second, widespread tax derogations, whether statutory or discretionary, have eroded the tax base and led to large shortfalls from targeted revenue levels. Third, the poor performance in revenue collection has brought to light considerable weaknesses in the tax and customs administrations. Fourth, because of the need for early and rapid deficit reduction, the reliance on export and import taxes has been useful or unavoidable in several cases—especially given the unexpectedly favorable export prices—but poses a risk for efficiency in the future, at least on its current scale.

Against this backdrop, a major effort is clearly needed to ensure a durable increase in revenue collection in terms of GDP. The challenge will therefore be not only to strengthen the tax and customs administrations but also to broaden the tax base and steer the tax structure toward more efficient expenditure-based taxes and modernized income tax regimes—which in turn would lessen the countries' dependence on international trade taxation.

In proceeding with these reforms, two principles will need to be kept in mind. Success in improving revenue performance depends first and foremost on political will, and not only on reforms of administration and instruments; this is particularly true when the issue is the elimination of exemptions and loopholes that benefit specific interests. Second, the tax system must remain simple and easily understood, which requires that tax reforms be preceded by adequate preparation, even in a period of pressing revenue needs.

Strengthening Tax and Customs Administrations

To restructure tax collecting agencies, a number of corrective measures, often already incorporated into existing programs, need to be effectively implemented or reinforced without delay in most CFA franc countries.[31] First, tax administration should focus on the largest taxpayers, either companies or individuals, because in most countries 80–90 percent of tax revenues are due from a limited number of easily identifiable taxpayers. To this end, it is important to establish a specialized unit for the monitoring of assessments and collections of taxes due. Second, the relations and communications between the domestic tax, customs, and treasury departments need to be improved, simplified, and tightly coordinated to facilitate the cross-checking of tax declarations. Third, the systematic registration and identification of taxpayers through a single identification number should be effected as early as possible. Fourth, administrative controls need to be reinforced through frequent in-house inspections, and tax officials offered incentives based on results. Finally, appropriate training in modern management techniques and upgrades in equipment are urgently required in many tax administrations.

The strengthening of customs administrations, where revenue shortfalls have been greatest in 1994, should be given high priority. Efforts need to be focused on improving clearance procedures (and tightening transitory regimes), as well as on controlling the value of imported goods. Import verification programs should be tightened in several countries, with support, as needed, from preshipment inspection companies. Moreover, appropriate measures to prevent fraud and parallel market activities should be given particular importance. The computerization of some critical tasks in the customs departments also has to be undertaken in those countries where this is made necessary by the volume of customs operations. These measures should be accompanied by the reinforcement of internal controls and sanctions, the strengthening of customs officials' incentive systems to combat fraud, and the reorganization of central offices to improve the transparency and efficiency of administrative operations.

[31]Fund technical assistance to CFA franc countries has been extensive in the last two years; it has sought to remedy weaknesses in tax and customs administrations and to simplify tax and tariff legislations. Technical assistance missions' recommendations have often been detailed in individual country reform programs. In addition to the posting of several long-term IMF technical assistance experts, specialized missions have assisted most countries in the BEAC subregion in the implementation of the CAECU reform, including the introduction of the VAT in Gabon. For details, see Annex IV on technical assistance.

Improving the Tax Base and Structure

The exemption from taxes of a wide array of economic operations has seriously eroded the *tax base* in recent years, and has contributed to a sharp fall in the tax revenue/GDP ratio in most CFA franc countries. Statutory or contractual tax exemptions were established during the period prior to the devaluation,[32] when increasingly fewer activities could be pursued profitably without special protection or exemptions to general tax regimes. Revenue forgone on account of these exemptions is estimated to have been in the range of 20–50 percent of potential tax receipts in recent years.[33] These exemptions have led the authorities to maintain relatively high tariff and tax rates on an increasingly smaller number of taxpayers or product categories, which in turn have tended to foster distortions, fraud, and misallocation of resources. Not infrequently, state monopolies have been granted exemptions under individual arrangements. There has also been a multiplication of exemptions on an ad hoc basis in several countries, with opportunities for arbitrariness and abuse in the administration of the tax system.

The reduction or elimination of these exemptions should therefore be at the core of tax reform efforts. Progress in this area needs to be made rapidly in most countries, and particularly in the CAEMC countries. Indeed, the CAECU customs tariff and indirect tax reform of June 1993 calls for all ad hoc exemptions—as well as those granted by investment codes and specific regimes or bilateral conventions—to be renegotiated or eliminated by end-1995.[34] A similar agreement at the regional level is needed in the WAEMU to prevent the undermining of efforts in one country by a greater tolerance for exceptions in another.[35]

The broadening of the tax base should also be sought through a more adequate taxation of small and medium-size companies, and of the informal sector. Although efforts to collect taxes from the largest companies should remain a priority, the taxation of these expanding sectors in most countries could draw useful lessons from the approach followed in Benin and Côte d'Ivoire. The mechanism that has been in place for some time in these two countries consists of substituting a single minimum fee (impôt synthétique), based on turnover or rent value, for ill-adapted taxes.

The broadening of the tax base should be paralleled and supported by adjustments in the *tax structure*, with a view to increasing reliance on expenditure-based taxes and domestic taxes and to reducing dependence on international trade taxation. The objectives should be to adjust the structure to reduce distortions, improve income distribution, and lessen the vulnerability of revenue to changes in the external environment. The reform of indirect, income and property, and export taxation therefore needs to be actively on the agenda for the next few years.

In reforming indirect taxation, the WAEMU and CAEMC countries will face different challenges, though both subregions have to take into account their current or future participation in a common trade area. In the CAEMC countries, efforts will need to continue to center on a determined implementation of the CAECU reform. The external (and intraregional) tariff has already been harmonized, entailing a reduction of nominal effective protection;[36] the new, two-tier (3–6 percent and 8–17 percent) domestic turnover tax (TCA) and excise taxes on a range of goods are now in place everywhere. In April 1995, however, Gabon moved directly to a value-added tax (VAT), a move that was originally scheduled to follow the introduction of the TCA by a few years, while Cameroon raised the upper rate of the lower tier to 8 percent and the upper rate of the upper tier TCA to 17 percent in June 1995. This suggests that there is a need for further coordination and harmonization within the CAEMC, but also that, with efficient management and collection of the TCA and excise taxes, the generalized move to a VAT can be envisaged in the not too distant future, once the preparatory work has been completed.

In the WAEMU, where the VAT is already in place in all countries, reforms should concentrate on the simplification and regional harmonization of the customs tariff and indirect tax rates, as part of the effort to establish a common market. The sequencing of the tariff and tax reforms, however, will have to be designed carefully, particularly because of the potential for revenue loss by landlocked countries.

The reform of income and property taxes is a longer-term proposition and, in some countries (Côte d'Ivoire, Cameroon, and Gabon), will greatly facilitate the necessary reduction in reliance on export taxes. Although the drawbacks of export taxation are recognized in all countries, the authorities

[32]Under investment codes or under individual arrangements (conventions d'établissement).

[33]During the period June 1993–June 1994, goods exempted from customs duties were estimated at 30–65 percent of imports in value terms in the CAEMC countries (see Annex II, Table 55).

[34]The agreement of June 1993 excludes exemptions granted under the Vienna Convention and public procurements. In these cases and in those of the NGOs, however, countries will need to tighten criteria and controls because of possible abuse.

[35]To the extent that exemptions have been granted under contractual agreements, the authorities may not be at liberty to revoke them unilaterally; the agreements may thus have to be allowed to run their course, before they can be renegotiated and the exemptions eliminated.

[36]See Annex II, Table 55. The intraregional tariff is also expected to be phased out by January 1, 1998.

are concerned that the alternatives raise difficult trade-offs and issues of design and management that most CFA franc countries are not equipped to address adequately—that is, without large revenue losses.[37] These difficulties, however, should not delay the progressive reduction of the rates of export taxation so that the wedge between domestic and foreign prices becomes less economically distorting; this reduction should be accompanied by efforts to rapidly modernize and simplify the system of personal or corporate income taxation[38] and broaden further the reach of domestic indirect taxes.

Expenditure Restraint and Management

To restore in due course a viable fiscal position, all CFA franc countries need to keep public sector spending in check, while reallocating expenditure away from the wage bill and toward physical infrastructure and human resource development.

Restraint in government total remuneration is, to be sure, crucial to overall fiscal adjustment and to maintaining cost control in the nontraded goods sector,[39] but it must not be achieved at any cost in terms of efficiency. At the same time, budget allocations need to be restored to appropriate levels for basic health, education, and infrastructure, as well as, where needed, for social safety net expenditures. In the context of its public expenditure reviews and its support to the formulation of public investment programs (PIPs), the World Bank is giving priority to these issues, and its views are being incorporated in the programs supported by the Fund.

Weaknesses also need to be addressed rapidly in public sector financial management. In addition to institutional capacity building and investment programming, there is a need to strengthen budget formulation to ensure unity and comprehensiveness, as well as effective treasury management, expenditure control, and accounting procedures. The management and supervision of autonomous public agencies and public enterprises also need to be strengthened, which will often require technical assistance from the donor community. In addition, the selection and monitoring of investment projects calls for urgent improvements, with greater attention to cost-benefit analysis, rates of return, the associated future recurrent expenditure, and the needs for counterpart funding. Finally, in a number of countries, public investment budgets will need to be made consistent with PIPs, and consolidated with the current budget, with due regard being paid to overall fiscal constraints and to recurrent cost implications.

[37]Either these alternatives are economically efficient, such as taxes based on land values or on imputed farm income, but difficult and costly to administer—because they require, for instance, detailed and frequently updated cadastral surveys and estimates of land profitability—or they are easy to implement, such as taxes on farm inputs, but yield little and can lead to cost and price distortions.

[38]It is recognized that some activities, such as the timber industry, remain difficult to bring even under these simplified regimes.

[39]Wage bills still approached or exceeded government revenue in Niger and the Congo in 1994, and few countries would currently meet the regional convergence criterion of 50 percent of revenue agreed in the WAEMU.

Monetary and Credit Policy

The monetary arrangements of the two subzones impose constraints on monetary policy, not only at the individual country level but also at the subregional level. The emergence of regional interbank and money markets, and the progressive move to indirect instruments of monetary management, have sharply reduced the scope for country-specific monetary and credit policies. In addition, the monetary authorities are facing increasing difficulties in determining the precise level of currency in circulation or reserve money at the individual country level, and therefore can only produce tentative (and often revisable) estimates of individual member country contributions to the consolidated net external position of each of the two central banks. These observations argue in favor of a monetary policy that is not only designed and conducted but also monitored at the regional level. The bilateral discussions that have been taking place on a semiannual basis between the Fund staff and the BCEAO and the BEAC may thus need to be given greater operational content, both from the standpoint of surveillance over policies in general and in particular in the context of use of Fund resources. In this regard, it would seem important that understandings be reached on projections of regional money demand in the two subzones and on the expansion in the two central banks' net domestic assets consistent with the objectives for regional expenditure growth and the banks' net foreign positions. These understandings would have to be translated (a) at the *regional level*, into objectives for net support of, or restrictions on, the lending capacity of commercial banks to the private sector; and (b) at the *individual country level*, into limits on net access by the governments not only to bank financing but, more narrowly, to financing by the central bank (irrespective of any margin that might be available under the statutory ceiling on advances).[40]

[40]An important issue for the future is whether or not the currency arrangements should require that the governments' overdraft facility be gradually eliminated and that the governments instead rely on normal domestic financing at market conditions (that is, through commercial banks or through bond or bill issues, which in turn would encourage the development of financial markets). Such a move, however, would call for the observance of strict objectives for the governments' primary balances, as well as for the strengthening of domestic debt management capacity.

Control over bank lending to the private sector—assuming that such control can be exercised effectively, that is, to the extent that banks do not have freedom to draw on foreign resources to finance domestic operations—in turn raises the question of whether policy instruments are adequate to achieve the objectives. As indicated in Annex III, the two central banks have not yet fully developed their array of indirect monetary instruments, while they have already eschewed the direct instruments of monetary management (such as country and individual bank refinancing ceilings) that they had relied on in the past.

Programs recently negotiated or currently under discussion with the Fund have sought to increase the leverage of the two central banks' lending capacity, expanding the scope of intervention to include (a) symmetrical credit auctions or reverse auctions of central bank bills, a first step toward full-fledged open market operations;[41] (b) market determination of interest rates in these interventions, which will require that the two central banks refrain from fixing both quantity and prices at the auctions or reverse auctions as at present; and (c) the activation and refinement of existing reserve requirements, as needed.

It remains the case, however, that the effectiveness of monetary policy may be undermined, in the WAEMU, by the option to redeem at par the bonds issued in the context of the securitization scheme; and, in the CAEMC, by the possibility of open-ended refinancing of medium-term credit, and the voluntary character of the special deposits. Accordingly, the need to substitute central bank bills of various maturities for the paper issued in the context of the securitization scheme in the WAEMU, and for the special deposits in the CAEMC, needs to be actively examined. Improvements in and activation of legal reserve requirements will also have to be reviewed, particularly the existing use of the securitized debt to meet required reserve ratios in the WAEMU. In the CAEMC, the medium-term refinancing window will need to be closed as soon as conditions permit.

Financial and Banking Reforms

In recent years, given the arrangements governing the CFA franc zone and the unavailability of spontaneous domestic or external financing, the possibility of financing fiscal imbalances was limited to the accumulation of external and domestic payments arrears. This disorderly process of financing prevailed in most countries until the devaluation and contributed to undermining the functioning of the banking systems in several countries, as first the public sector and then its suppliers ceased meeting their financial obligations. A web of payments arrears was created, including arrears to commercial banks. As a result, most banking systems in the zone had turned both illiquid and insolvent by 1989–90 and had to undergo major restructurings.

These efforts led to measurable improvements in bank liquidity and solvency in both unions even before the devaluation; and, as expected, the restoration of liquidity has been helped greatly in 1994 by the rapid reconstitution of real money balances. Solvency has improved in most banking systems of the WAEMU; but progress has been uneven in the CAEMC, and substantial problems remain. Continued efforts are thus needed to strengthen the regional banking commissions and step up the necessary audits, liquidate insolvent banks, and recapitalize those in difficulty.[42] Although now reduced in scope, the problem of nonperforming loans to public enterprises also remains unsolved in certain countries, partly because interenterprise debts and cross-debts with governments have not been fully accounted for, let alone settled. Alongside the settlement of government arrears, effective public enterprise reforms thus remain a condition for restoring health to the financial sector.

While specific cases of troubled banks must surely be addressed, an important challenge now facing most countries and the two central banks is to strengthen and deepen financial intermediation and reduce intermediation costs. The objective is to enable the banking sector to play a larger role in mobilizing financial savings and supporting economic activity. Improving intermediation, however, hinges on providing a predictable legal and regulatory framework that allows banks to pursue their claims on borrowers and to exercise guarantees as needed. Accordingly, buttressing the judiciary through training, elimination of political interferences, and restoration of adequate compensation levels and pay relativities is becoming an integral part of the efforts to strengthen the financial systems.

The deepening of financial intermediation is recognized as a more protracted undertaking. For one thing, it requires creating the conditions, including fiscal consolidation and elimination of government arrears, for the progressive emergence of regional financial markets in which public debt instruments

[41] Treasury bill auctions may probably have to be ruled out as long as the regular servicing of the existing domestic debt has not been resumed (and domestic arrears have not been eliminated).

[42] Outright liquidations appear to be necessary only rarely. The authorities are developing, with World Bank support, solutions that involve either liquidations (that is, takeovers by other banks of the salvageable part of the portfolio) or the entry of new shareholders into the equity capital. To the extent possible, these solutions seek to minimize fiscal costs to the governments, except in those cases where state participation in the recapitalization is a condition for private shareholders to contribute to the operation.

can be traded. It also requires building on ongoing initiatives, especially in the countryside—where barter and cash-based exchange dominate—to set up or develop credit cooperatives or other systems of mutual credit. Similar arrangements are needed to support the growth of the small and medium-size enterprise sector, which often faces considerable difficulties accessing formal bank credit. Initiatives in this direction might involve building on such arrangements as the *tontine* credit networks, or introducing mechanisms akin to those successfully tested in Bangladesh (Grameen banks). Savings and loan type networks for the financing of social housing also need to be encouraged.

Structural Policies

In all CFA franc countries there is an urgent need for stepping up structural reforms. This will enhance the credibility of the adjustment strategy and create an environment where the private sector can take full advantage of the window of opportunity opened by the devaluation. At the same time, however, there is a need for a sharper prioritization of the critical mass of reforms that would take due account of the limitations of existing administrative capacity at both the national and the regional levels.

The reforms that were developed in the wake of the exchange rate action, but unevenly implemented in 1994, have centered on the progressive disengagement of the state from production activities that can be carried out more effectively by the private sector. They have also involved domestic deregulation and trade reforms, so as to increase efficiency further and reduce distortions. By making the economies more competitive internationally, these reforms will help integrate the zone in the mainstream of international trade and reduce its dependence on primary commodity exports. The agenda for the period ahead needs to impart greater momentum to this process.

Price liberalization has been at the core of the effort to increase flexibility in the economies of the zone, and ensure that international price signals are properly transmitted to domestic producers. Although producer prices have been greatly liberalized in many countries, not all have engineered a full pass-through of the devaluation to producers; state marketing boards remain active, notably in Benin, Mali, Côte d'Ivoire, and Senegal, although their activities have already been scaled down; and export taxes continue to act as a wedge between foreign and domestic prices.[43] At the consumer level, measures need to be taken to reduce the list of the remaining administered prices in a number of countries, and to ensure that public monopoly prices cover costs. Meanwhile, automatic rate adjustment mechanisms for electricity, water, telecommunications, and public transportation, and, as a first step, systems linking petroleum pump prices to world prices (already adopted by Côte d'Ivoire, Mali, and Senegal, among others) would need to be extended to other countries.

Liberalization of *labor markets* is lagging behind in most countries, except Cameroon, Chad, and Senegal. Measurable improvements are required in this area to lessen market rigidities and reduce the social costs of adjustment. Reforms of labor codes, and of labor legislation more generally, also need to be given greater impetus.

Updating and harmonizing *regulatory and legal frameworks*, at both the national and the regional levels, are under way. A few countries of the zone have not yet ratified the regional treaties on social security institutions, harmonization of statistics, and harmonization of business law (OHADA). The regional Court of Law, to be established by OHADA when it becomes operational, is expected to impart greater independence to judges and facilitate the enforcement of court decisions.

Privatization and restructuring of *public enterprises* experienced delays in 1994, as noted earlier. This process now has to be given stronger momentum, and the World Bank is placing increased priority to supporting it. The key objectives are to foster competition and sound management, raise economic efficiency and weaken opportunities for rents, and reduce the burden of subsidies on the government budgets.

Economic integration has received a boost from the devaluation, with the recognition that the currency area, to be viable over the long run, needs to be grounded in an equivalent economic area with goods and factor mobility, and a high degree of convergence of economic and policy performance.[44] However, the pace of implementation of the objectives envisaged in the treaties creating the WAEMU and the CAEMC has been uneven.[45] The WAEMU has taken the lead in moving toward regional surveillance, but has made only limited progress toward building a customs, let alone an economic, union. The CAEMC, for its part, has made important strides toward establishing a common market, with

[43]The measure has been deliberate in the case of cocoa in Côte d'Ivoire because of the latter's market-maker position and the need to encourage diversification of agricultural output.

[44]In addition, the need to deal with other barriers such as transport barriers, roadblocks, and similar formal and informal impediments to cross-border trade will have to continue to be addressed.

[45]The key objectives are the establishment of two common markets based on customs unions, the harmonization of indirect tax legislation, the coordination of economic policies among member countries through multilateral surveillance, and the implementation of common sectoral policies; see Annex II.

the adoption in the framework of the CAECU of the common external and intraregional tariff and of a common system of domestic indirect taxation. It has yet to agree, however, on the elements of the conventions on economic and monetary union (including the coverage and mechanism of regional surveillance) that are to flesh out the CAEMC treaty.

The WAEMU member countries must therefore be encouraged to move in due course to a common external tariff. In the CAEMC, the challenge ahead is to eliminate the loopholes provided by statutory or contractual exemptions, and to avoid granting new ad hoc exemptions. Although these actions are provided for in the CAECU decisions of June 1993, the experience of 1994 suggests that they will require firm resolve on the part of the authorities.

Regional surveillance, as provided for in the WAEMU treaty and the draft CAEU and CAMU conventions now under discussion in the CAEMC, needs to be encouraged to foster sound and mutually supportive economic and sectoral policies in the two subregions, as well as a better coordination of economic policies. Convergence indicators and appropriate policy coordination mechanisms should be supported by efforts at harmonizing public finance statistics, as well as budget laws and procedures.

Finally, to give a boost to the credibility of their strategy and reaffirm the outward-oriented character of the zone, the CFA franc countries should consider moving rapidly toward acceptance of the obligations of Article VIII, Sections 2, 3, and 4 of the Fund's Articles of Agreement.

Social Policies

On the social front, the implementation of social safety nets has varied widely from country to country. With the removal of the limits on price increases imposed on a few key consumer goods following the parity change, there is now a need to accelerate the implementation of well-targeted measures. This would help in alleviating the hardship on the poorest segments of the population, particularly in the cities. More generally, however, emergency social protection measures must progressively give way to lasting initiatives aimed at improving socioeconomic conditions. Accordingly, budgetary allocation decisions should place increased emphasis on the development of human resources, particularly health and primary education, and on essential economic infrastructure. This redirection of public expenditure would help in achieving sustainable economic growth and poverty reduction. In this context, public expenditure reviews, which are carried out with the help of the World Bank, should become a central element of the economic strategy of the member countries.

External Debt Management

Since early 1994, most CFA franc countries have benefited from substantial concessional reschedulings by Paris Club creditors, as well as from debt cancellation by several bilateral creditors (most notably, France). As noted above, eleven CFA franc countries have concessional rescheduling agreements currently in place—or lapsed—that envisage stock-of-debt operations over the next two and a half years. Under current Paris Club practices, these would be under Naples terms, provided the countries concerned establish track records of adjustment and good performance under the rescheduling agreements.[46] Such stock-of-debt operations, combined with comparable treatment by other bilateral and commercial creditors, should lead to a marked improvement in these countries' external debt situations. However, progress toward external viability will also require the pursuit of appropriate financial and structural adjustment policies to boost growth and export recovery, as well as continued external financial assistance on highly concessional terms.

In all CFA franc countries, a substantial improvement in the public finances will be a key condition to strengthening the external position over the medium term. Moreover, to improve debt-service profiles and lower average interest costs, these countries will have to resort primarily to grants and to long-term loans on highly concessional terms. Although most CFA franc countries have by and large regularized their relations with official bilateral creditors, administrative shortcomings have in some cases led to delays in meeting scheduled debt-service obligations. These shortcomings need to be addressed, as a matter of urgency in a number of cases, in the context of improvements in external debt management.

Overall, the timely and determined implementation of the policies and reforms envisaged in the adjustment programs, stock-of-debt operations tailored to the countries' capacity to meet their foreign financial obligations, and appropriate new financing on concessional terms should permit a lasting exit from the rescheduling process and the achievement of external debt sustainability for eligible CFA franc countries. In the cases of Cameroon, the Congo, and Côte d'Ivoire, Paris Club action will need to be complemented by agreement on a menu of debt or debt-service reduction options with foreign commercial banks that are consistent with these countries' ability to pay.

[46]Benin, Burkina Faso, Cameroon, the C.A.R,, Chad, Côte d'Ivoire, Equatorial Guinea, Mali, Niger, Senegal, and Togo. The Congo and Gabon had nonconcessional reschedulings.

V Conclusions

The CFA franc countries have largely met in 1994 the objectives of the programs they had developed in the aftermath of the devaluation of the CFA franc with regard to economic growth, inflation, and the external position. Furthermore, with restraint in wage policy, competitiveness has been restored. Performance, however, has been uneven in the two crucial areas of fiscal adjustment and structural reforms, which need to be enhanced to ensure the sustainability of the recovery and the return to external viability.

Overall, the economic policy mix envisaged in the medium-term strategy, aimed at validating the new level of the exchange rate anchor and at sparking the recovery of the economies of the zone, remains appropriate. However, contrary to program intentions, the brunt of fiscal adjustment in the first year fell disproportionately on nonwage primary expenditure and on capital outlays, as there were sizable shortfalls in tax revenue in most countries. This fiscal policy mix is not sustainable and, with the slow initial implementation of structural reforms, suggests that corrective actions are needed to keep the adjustment strategy on course. Thus, the member countries of the CFA franc zone should take advantage of the generally favorable international environment to consolidate and deepen their adjustment efforts and to implement a critical mass of structural measures that would create an environment conducive to sustainable growth with financial stability.

For the immediate future, the primary concern is to strengthen policy performance in the countries where program implementation has been weak following the devaluation. This calls first for a correction of the government revenue shortfalls experienced by several countries in 1994. The reform of customs regimes and of domestic indirect taxation is now in place in the CAEMC, and is under discussion in the WAEMU. The objective is to broaden the tax base and curb the incidence of exemptions, while reducing effective protection. But, the effect of these reforms will depend on the determination of the authorities to carry them through by strengthening the tax collection agencies and mechanisms, reducing exemptions and refraining from granting new ones, and fighting fraud and illicit practices.

A structure of government revenue less vulnerable to external shocks, however, must be the long-term aim of the reforms to be undertaken in the period ahead. Extensive Fund technical assistance has already been, or is being, provided in the design and implementation of the CAECU and WAEMU customs tariff and indirect tax reforms. It will also be needed, along with that of other donors, in designing plans of action in other areas of revenue mobilization, including tax administration. Another central issue of policy will be that of gradually reducing and eventually eliminating reliance on export taxes, and replacing them with workable mechanisms of income (or imputed income) or land taxation. In this area, however, improvements will necessarily be slow to come by. Work on strengthening the existing domestic revenue base—involving simple and easy-to-administer taxation regimes for the informal sector, and concentration on the taxpayers responsible for the bulk of economic activity—must therefore remain the central task in the short run.

As regards government expenditure, the authorities need to ensure that outlays on social safety net measures and basic social services are preserved or increased as planned, and that greater attention is given to the programming and implementation of public investment. At the same time, expenditure policies should take account of the evolving revenue situation to avoid any backsliding on consolidating budgetary positions. The authorities need to, as a matter of priority, guard against relaxing public wage policy. They should therefore pursue efforts vigorously to bring the civil service to an efficient size. This is essential not only to improve pay relativities in the administrations but also to achieve the desired restructuring of public expenditure in favor of investment in human and physical capital.

Another key challenge is to step up structural reform efforts so as to build on the gains in competitiveness permitted by the devaluation and create the conditions for self-sustained growth. Governments will need first to strengthen public sector administrative capacity. Priority areas already identified include public expenditure reviews, civil service reform, strict project selection under public investment programs, health and education sector development, and public enterprise reform.

The authorities should also promptly put in place reforms that support a strong private sector capable of becoming the true engine of economic growth. The measures required here are the acceleration of state enterprise privatization; the liberalization of remaining controls on prices, labor markets, and external and domestic commercial activity; and the completion of the restructuring of the financial sectors. At the same time, the authorities need to continue to work at the regional level to deepen financial intermediation and to improve the instruments of monetary policy at the disposal of the two central banks, in order to increase reliance on market mechanisms and to promote saving mobilization and appropriate allocation of financial resources. The pursuit of these reforms should be supported by the adoption of a stable and predictable legal framework that encourages private sector initiative and strengthens investor confidence. In that connection, the CFA franc countries have recently taken a decision to accept the obligations of Article VIII, Sections 2, 3, and 4 of the Fund's Articles of Agreement.

The CFA franc countries will need to sustain and deepen their adjustment efforts so as to enhance saving rates and their debt-servicing capacity. Meanwhile, sound borrowing policy would mean reliance mainly on grants or on loans on highly concessional terms. With programs carefully adhered to, debt-stock operations under the auspices of the Paris Club, appropriately tailored to the countries' capacity to pay, will help alleviate the existing debt burden. Solutions with similar effects will need to be developed with private creditors by the countries, such as Côte d'Ivoire, the Congo, and Cameroon, that have sizable debts to the market.

Finally, the two subregions need to intensify the momentum of regional integration and economic cooperation. This would help avoid inconsistent policies. It would also facilitate the emergence of large economic areas that offer broader markets and opportunities for economies of scale, and encourage factor mobility. The development of the regional instruments of surveillance to foster economic convergence therefore should be actively encouraged. Appropriate use of these instruments would greatly improve the chances for a virtuous circle of sound macroeconomic policies, increased saving mobilization, proper resource allocation, and sustainable economic growth rates.

Annex I Statistical Tables

Table 3. Nominal GDP, 1990–96
(Annual percentage changes)

	1990–93 Average	1990	1991	1992	1993	1994 Original program	1994 Provi-sional	1994 Deviation	1995 Program/ Projections	1996 Projections
WAEMU	–0.2	–2.0	0.7	1.6	–1.0	39.1	38.5	–0.6	14.8	9.0
Benin	5.9	4.8	6.6	6.6	5.4	29.5	40.4	10.9	22.0	6.9
Burkina Faso	1.4	–0.1	4.5	0.6	0.6	32.0	29.4	–2.6	14.3	10.3
Côte d'Ivoire	–2.9	–9.8	–0.1	–0.3	–1.5	41.8	42.1	0.3	14.4	9.4
Mali	3.7	3.2	–0.3	9.7	2.3	38.4	37.8	–0.6	13.6	8.5
Niger	–2.5	–2.9	–2.8	–5.5	1.3	36.0	36.0	0.0	11.5	7.4
Senegal	1.9	5.2	–0.2	4.1	–1.6	42.8	35.8	–7.0	12.6	7.3
Togo	–3.0	3.2	2.2	–1.8	–15.4	40.4	43.9	3.5	21.0	16.3
CAEMC	–1.2	1.9	–1.3	–2.0	–3.6	32.9	38.0	5.1	12.3	8.8
Cameroon	–3.5	–1.1	–4.4	–2.3	–6.1	30.3	39.4	9.1	15.9	8.6
Central African Republic	–2.7	0.3	–4.8	–3.4	–2.9	41.5	36.5	–5.0	19.4	9.7
Chad	–1.4	–0.8	8.8	1.0	–14.4	33.6	49.0	15.4	12.9	9.4
Congo	–0.1	0.4	0.8	0.7	–2.2	24.4	21.4	–3.0	1.0	17.8
Equatorial Guinea	5.7	0.8	2.2	14.1	5.5	52.8	42.7	–10.2	15.2	10.4
Gabon	3.3	10.6	3.1	–3.6	3.0	38.8	40.3	1.5	7.5	5.1
Zone	–0.7	–0.2	–0.2	–0.1	–2.2	36.4	38.3	1.9	13.7	8.9
Comoros	2.9	4.7	2.9	1.2	2.7	12.0	23.8	11.8	6.4	7.1

Sources: Data provided by the authorities; and Fund staff estimates and projections as of the end of May 1995.

Table 4. Real Rate of Growth, 1990–96

(Annual percentage changes)

	1990–93 Average	1990	1991	1992	1993	1994 Original program	1994 Provisional	1994 Deviation	1995 Program/ Projections	1996 Projections
WAEMU[1]	0.3	0.2	0.9	1.2	−1.2	2.5	2.6	0.1	5.5	5.6
Benin	3.8	3.1	4.7	4.1	3.2	2.2	3.4	1.2	6.3	5.6
Burkina Faso	2.6	−1.5	10.0	2.5	−0.8	3.3	1.2	−2.1	5.3	5.1
Côte d'Ivoire	−0.9	−2.1	−0.8	—	−0.8	0.8	1.7	0.9	6.4	6.7
Mali	1.2	0.4	−2.5	7.8	−0.8	2.4	2.4	—	5.1	4.8
Niger	−1.0	−1.3	2.5	−6.5	1.4	3.9	4.0	0.1	4.2	4.2
Senegal	1.1	4.5	−0.7	2.8	−2.1	2.7	2.0	−0.7	4.5	4.7
Togo	−4.5	0.1	−0.9	−3.7	−13.5	11.7	10.7	−1.0	5.7	6.0
CAEMC[1]	−1.2	−1.8	−1.5	0.4	−2.1	−1.1	−0.4	0.7	4.2	5.6
Cameroon	−4.4	−5.6	−7.3	−0.8	−4.0	−2.4	−1.1	1.3	5.6	6.4
Central African Republic	−1.6	−1.0	−0.6	−2.5	−2.2	5.5	6.7	1.2	4.1	4.9
Chad	1.8	−2.3	13.2	8.0	−11.9	1.4	4.0	2.6	5.4	4.9
Congo	1.0	0.6	2.2	2.4	−1.2	−2.4	−6.7	−4.3	0.3	7.7
Equatorial Guinea	5.6	3.3	−1.1	13.0	7.1	8.9	2.5	−6.4	8.6	6.7
Gabon	3.5	5.4	5.0	0.5	2.9	−0.8	1.1	1.9	2.6	3.1
Zone[1]	−0.4	−0.7	−0.2	0.8	−1.6	1.0	1.3	0.3	5.0	5.6
Comoros	1.9	2.5	2.1	1.6	1.3	0.7	0.8	0.1	2.2	3.0

Sources: Data provided by the authorities; and Fund staff estimates and projections as of the end of May 1995.
[1]Weighted average using the corresponding GDP of the respective countries.

Table 5. GDP Deflator, 1990–96

(Annual percentage changes)

	1990–93 Average	1990	1991	1992	1993	1994 Original program	1994 Provisional	1994 Deviation	1995 Program/ Projections	1996 Projections
WAEMU[1]	−0.4	−2.3	−0.1	0.5	0.3	35.2	35.0	−0.2	8.7	3.2
Benin	1.9	1.2	1.9	2.4	2.1	24.7	35.7	11.0	14.8	1.2
Burkina Faso	−1.0	1.4	−5.0	−1.8	1.4	27.7	27.9	0.2	8.6	5.0
Côte d'Ivoire	−2.0	−7.9	0.7	−0.3	−0.6	41.2	39.6	−1.6	7.6	2.6
Mali	2.4	2.9	2.1	1.9	2.6	35.1	34.5	−0.6	8.0	3.5
Niger	−1.4	−1.6	−5.1	1.1	−0.1	30.9	30.8	−0.1	7.0	2.9
Senegal	0.7	0.6	0.5	1.2	0.4	35.4	33.2	−2.2	7.8	2.5
Togo	1.5	3.1	3.2	1.8	−2.2	29.2	30.2	1.0	14.4	9.7
CAEMC[1]	−0.1	2.9	0.5	−2.4	−1.3	33.9	38.4	4.5	7.7	3.2
Cameroon	0.7	3.1	3.1	−1.5	−2.1	33.5	40.9	7.4	9.7	2.1
Central African Republic	−1.0	1.9	−4.2	−0.9	−0.7	36.1	27.9	−8.2	14.7	4.6
Chad	−2.9	1.6	−3.9	−6.5	−2.8	31.8	43.3	11.5	7.0	4.3
Congo	−1.1	−0.2	−1.4	−1.6	−1.0	27.4	30.0	2.6	0.7	9.4
Equatorial Guinea	0.1	−2.5	3.5	0.9	−1.5	40.2	39.1	−1.1	6.1	3.5
Gabon	−0.2	4.9	−1.8	−4.1	0.2	36.9	38.7	1.8	4.7	2.0
Zone[1]	−0.2	0.2	0.2	−0.8	−0.4	34.7	36.5	1.8	8.3	3.2
Comoros	1.0	2.2	0.8	−0.4	1.4	12.5	22.8	10.3	4.1	3.9

Sources: Data provided by the authorities; and Fund staff estimates and projections as of the end of May 1995.
[1]Weighted average using the corresponding GDP of the respective countries.

Table 6. Inflation (CPI), 1990–96
(Percentage changes, annual average)

	1990–93 Average	1990	1991	1992	1993	1994 Original program	1994 Provi-sional	1994 Deviation	1995 Program/ Projections	1996 Projections
WAEMU[1]	0.5	–0.2	0.6	1.2	0.5	31.9	29.7	–2.2	9.6	3.4
Benin	2.4	1.1	2.1	5.9	0.5	26.0	38.6	12.6	15.9	4.0
Burkina Faso	0.1	–0.8	2.5	–2.0	0.6	31.2	24.7	–6.5	7.9	3.9
Côte d'Ivoire	1.8	–0.7	1.6	4.2	2.2	26.2	25.8	–0.4	8.0	3.2
Mali	–0.9	1.6	1.5	–5.9	–0.6	40.1	25.3	–14.8	8.0	3.5
Niger	–1.5	–2.0	–1.9	–1.7	–0.4	31.1	35.6	4.5	13.7	4.7
Senegal	–0.6	0.3	–1.8	–0.1	–0.6	39.1	32.1	–7.0	7.8	2.5
Togo	0.4	1.0	0.4	3.7	–3.6	35.9	41.4	5.5	16.9	4.0
CAEMC[1]	–0.4	1.4	1.5	–2.7	–1.7	33.3	37.3	4.0	10.2	3.6
Cameroon	–0.7	–0.5	1.0	–0.2	–3.2	31.0	34.5	3.5	10.3	3.6
Central African Republic	–1.7	–0.2	–2.8	–0.8	–2.9	35.0	24.5	–10.5	21.3	3.4
Chad	–1.6	0.5	4.0	–3.8	–7.0	43.3	41.3	–2.0	6.5	4.5
Congo	2.0	2.6	1.5	2.2	1.8	40.3	56.9	16.6	10.5	2.8
Equatorial Guinea	–0.5	0.7	–3.4	–4.3	5.2	35.2	40.6	5.4	8.6	4.4
Gabon	–0.3	5.7	3.3	–10.8	0.6	31.7	36.1	4.4	8.0	3.8
Zone[1]	0.1	0.6	1.0	–0.6	–0.5	32.5	33.0	0.6	9.9	3.5
Comoros	1.1	2.0	1.7	–1.4	1.9	15.0	25.6	10.6	4.8	3.5

Sources: Data provided by the authorities; and Fund staff estimates and projections as of the end of May 1995.
[1]Weighted average using the corresponding GDP of the respective countries.

Table 7. Cumulative Consumer Price Index, 1994 and 1995 (January–June)[1]

(December 1993 = 100)

	1994												1995						
	Jan.	Feb.	Mar.	Apr.	May	June	July	Aug.	Sept.	Oct.	Nov.	Dec.	Jan.	Feb.	Mar.	April	May	June	Dec. 94/May 95 (Percentage change)
WAEMU[2]	108.8	117.6	122.5	125.0	127.2	129.5	132.4	134.2	135.1	136.7	137.0	136.3	138.4	138.9	141.6	142.5	143.8	...	5.5
Benin	119.3	126.2	131.5	137.6	135.4	133.6	135.1	133.9	141.6	144.6	147.8	154.3	153.3	152.5	154.9	156.9	159.1	154.6	3.1
Burkina Faso	106.2	114.0	115.6	122.5	123.5	127.9	124.5	126.2	129.0	128.3	131.1	129.1	129.1	128.9	128.9	131.0	131.0	133.0	1.5
Côte d'Ivoire	108.2	114.4	120.0	121.5	124.8	128.2	130.3	130.6	131.5	131.9	131.8	131.9	138.7	139.2	143.4	144.7	146.0	146.9	10.7
Mali	109.7	117.2	117.7	121.1	122.9	128.7	132.3	134.2	134.2	134.2	134.0	132.1	130.8	133.4	134.8	137.5	143.3	141.6	8.5
Niger	101.1	114.0	126.7	128.8	134.0	137.7	140.9	141.9	140.0	138.8	142.8	140.6	140.3	140.1	142.1	141.1	144.2	148.3	2.6
Senegal	110.4	121.5	126.0	126.7	128.1	127.2	134.3	140.0	139.5	144.6	141.0	137.5	135.0	135.9	138.8	138.2	136.8	139.7	-0.5
Togo	105.9	123.6	127.0	128.7	131.8	132.1	137.7	139.5	138.7	142.8	147.5	148.4	152.9	152.7	152.7	153.2	154.0	...	3.8
CAEMC[2]	109.0	123.7	129.9	132.3	133.7	137.5	139.8	144.9	148.1	145.5	147.5	149.6	153.5	152.2	151.6	...	...	...	...
Cameroon	107.0	123.4	128.6	129.0	128.6	132.0	134.4	138.9	145.7	144.5	147.8	148.4	153.3	150.6	150.8	151.1	151.2	...	1.9
Central Afric. Rep.	100.4	110.1	111.6	117.9	121.7	131.9	136.7	136.0	135.6	134.6	143.1	144.7	152.3	151.6	152.2	150.1	...	...	...
Chad	104.2	120.4	133.9	145.4	150.1	152.7	151.8	156.8	156.6	153.3	151.3	149.4	152.9	154.2	151.7	149.9	150.3	158.8	0.6
Congo	125.2	135.0	144.9	143.5	147.3	151.5	155.9	162.5	163.9	159.0	163.1	164.1	175.9	176.8	172.0	...	...	...	...
Equatorial Guinea[3]	123.3	126.3	128.7	135.8	137.6	140.5	140.7	144.2	148.9	144.1	144.7	145.2	143.6	145.1	147.0	145.1	144.5	...	-0.5
Gabon	108.4	123.1	129.4	134.0	136.5	139.8	141.4	148.2	146.7	146.9	144.7	146.9	145.7	145.2	144.9	149.1	152.8	153.4	4.0
Zone[2]	108.9	120.3	125.8	128.2	130.0	133.0	135.7	138.9	140.8	141.1	142.1	142.2	145.0	144.7	145.9	...	...	...	...
Comoros	97.7	103.9	93.4	97.8	100.5	100.3	104.5	107.8	126.9	132.4	124.0	125.0	135.0	136.8	131.7	...	...	...	...

Sources: Data provided by the authorities; and Fund staff estimates and projections as of the end of May 1995.

[1]End-of-period basis.

[2]Weighted average using 1994 (provisional estimates) and 1995 (program/projections) GDP.

[3]Provisional for 1995; official data from the continental portion of Equatorial Guinea not yet available.

Table 8. Total Consumption, 1990–96

(In percent of GDP)

	1990–93 Average	1990	1991	1992	1993	1994 Original program	1994 Provi-sional	1994 Deviation	1995 Program/ Projections	1996 Projections
WAEMU	90.6	89.9	89.7	90.5	92.5	86.4	86.0	–0.5	84.3	83.3
Benin	94.8	94.5	94.0	95.6	95.1	93.6	90.5	–3.1	90.6	89.2
Burkina Faso	94.1	91.7	95.4	95.1	94.4	93.2	93.9	0.7	94.0	92.7
Côte d'Ivoire	85.0	85.7	83.6	83.5	87.3	73.5	73.2	–0.3	72.0	72.5
Mali	93.6	93.8	92.9	94.8	92.9	96.1	94.6	–1.6	90.9	89.8
Niger	96.4	96.0	92.5	98.2	98.7	99.0	99.3	0.3	98.2	96.2
Senegal	92.7	91.3	93.3	92.4	93.8	90.6	91.6	1.0	88.7	86.9
Togo	93.4	86.9	90.6	92.9	103.2	97.3	92.9	–4.4	88.2	84.8
CAEMC	80.3	79.4	79.5	81.8	80.7	75.1	70.1	–5.0	70.6	69.8
Cameroon	84.3	83.8	83.5	85.7	84.3	82.7	77.1	–5.6	75.4	73.9
Central African Republic	98.0	98.9	96.9	99.9	96.3	94.0	92.3	–1.7	93.0	91.9
Chad	109.4	104.0	111.1	111.1	111.5	109.8	102.7	–7.2	103.2	104.9
Congo	82.2	78.4	81.4	79.1	90.0	73.0	72.7	–0.3	74.4	67.9
Equatorial Guinea	89.9	89.2	85.3	97.1	88.0	77.7	75.9	–1.7	80.8	77.2
Gabon	60.0	59.2	58.6	63.0	59.3	51.5	43.7	–7.8	46.1	47.7
Zone	86.0	85.0	85.1	86.6	87.3	81.7	79.0	–2.7	78.3	77.4
Comoros	101.8	105.4	103.7	99.3	98.9	101.6	95.4	–6.2	96.0	94.3

Sources: Data provided by the authorities and Fund staff estimates and projections as of the end of May 1995.

Table 9. Total Gross Domestic Investment, 1990–96

(In percent of GDP)

	1990–93 Average	1990	1991	1992	1993	1994 Original program	1994 Provi-sional	1994 Deviation	1995 Program/ Projections	1996 Projections
WAEMU	13.5	13.6	13.8	13.9	12.5	18.0	15.7	–2.2	16.7	18.0
Benin	14.4	14.2	14.5	13.9	14.9	21.4	14.3	–7.1	15.2	16.6
Burkina Faso	21.7	20.4	20.9	21.6	23.7	31.9	25.3	–6.6	23.7	24.4
Côte d'Ivoire	9.7	8.8	10.7	10.9	8.4	14.0	14.1	0.1	14.9	16.4
Mali	22.3	22.4	23.1	21.9	21.9	26.9	26.5	–0.4	26.0	26.5
Niger	7.1	8.1	9.2	5.4	5.7	12.1	8.3	–3.8	10.1	11.4
Senegal	13.2	13.6	12.3	14.0	13.2	16.2	13.7	–2.5	15.6	17.1
Togo	15.7	24.9	17.5	16.3	3.9	12.5	10.9	–1.6	15.4	17.1
CAEMC	17.5	18.7	18.5	16.2	16.6	19.6	19.5	–0.2	20.8	21.9
Cameroon	15.4	17.4	16.0	14.3	14.1	13.2	15.8	2.6	18.0	19.8
Central African Republic	13.2	14.2	13.4	13.1	12.3	15.1	14.0	–1.1	15.0	15.2
Chad	11.4	18.7	7.9	8.4	10.6	14.9	14.3	–0.5	13.7	14.5
Congo	16.3	16.7	18.9	15.8	13.8	33.5	21.8	–11.7	20.8	22.1
Equatorial Guinea	31.1	26.7	43.2	24.3	30.2	23.9	41.9	18.0	32.6	21.1
Gabon	24.4	23.8	26.5	22.8	24.5	26.4	27.0	0.6	29.2	29.8
Zone	15.3	16.0	16.0	14.9	14.3	18.7	17.4	–1.3	18.5	19.7
Comoros	17.4	20.2	14.5	20.3	14.6	20.3	21.4	1.1	19.0	19.5

Sources: Data provided by the authorities; and Fund staff estimates and projections as of the end of May 1995.

Table 10. Gross Public Investment, 1990–96
(In percent of GDP)

	1990–93 Average	1990	1991	1992	1993	1994 Original program	1994 Provisional	1994 Deviation	1995 Program/ Projections	1996 Projections
WAEMU	5.0	4.9	5.1	5.3	4.9	7.4	6.2	–1.2	6.6	6.9
Benin	7.1	7.4	7.5	6.7	6.7	10.7	9.5	–1.2	9.8	8.8
Burkina Faso	6.9	4.3	6.4	8.9	8.0	12.0	7.0	–5.0	8.3	8.6
Côte d'Ivoire	3.2	2.8	3.2	3.3	3.4	5.2	5.2	—	5.4	5.8
Mali	10.4	10.3	12.3	9.7	9.3	13.7	12.8	–0.9	12.8	12.5
Niger	4.8	7.4	3.7	3.9	4.2	9.4	4.8	–4.6	5.6	6.4
Senegal	4.5	4.1	4.6	5.1	4.1	4.9	4.6	–0.3	4.8	5.1
Togo	4.2	7.2	4.5	3.5	1.6	3.1	2.2	–0.9	3.9	4.6
CAEMC	4.5	5.3	4.3	4.1	4.4	5.6	3.5	–2.2	4.0	4.4
Cameroon	4.3	5.6	4.2	3.7	3.9	3.3	1.7	–1.6	2.0	2.3
Central African Republic	7.2	7.1	7.7	7.4	6.8	8.6	7.6	–1.0	8.4	8.3
Chad	10.8	18.2	7.5	7.9	9.9	13.8	13.3	–0.5	12.3	12.1
Congo	1.5	2.7	0.9	0.8	1.7	8.0	3.1	–4.9	2.7	4.8
Equatorial Guinea	16.4	17.5	16.6	16.2	15.3	11.8	7.1	–4.7	9.8	8.7
Gabon	4.0	2.4	4.4	4.5	4.7	5.6	3.8	–1.8	5.4	5.5
Zone	4.8	5.1	4.8	4.7	4.7	6.6	5.0	–1.6	5.5	5.8
Comoros	7.3	5.3	5.7	10.4	7.7	9.9	9.6	–0.4	7.2	6.8

Sources: Data provided by the authorities; and Fund staff estimates and projections as of the end of May 1995.
Note: Including investments of public enterprises.

Table 11. Total Private Investment, 1990–96
(In percent of GDP)

	1990–93 Average	1990	1991	1992	1993	1994 Original program	1994 Provisional	1994 Deviation	1995 Program/ Projections	1996 Projections
WAEMU	8.4	8.6	8.7	8.6	7.7	10.6	9.5	–1.0	10.1	11.2
Benin	7.3	6.8	7.0	7.2	8.2	10.7	4.8	–5.9	5.4	7.7
Burkina Faso	14.7	16.1	14.5	12.6	15.7	19.9	18.3	–1.6	15.4	15.8
Côte d'Ivoire	6.5	6.0	7.5	7.6	5.1	8.8	8.9	0.1	9.5	10.6
Mali	11.9	12.1	10.8	12.2	12.6	13.3	13.7	0.5	13.2	14.0
Niger	2.3	0.7	5.5	1.5	1.5	2.7	3.5	0.8	4.5	5.0
Senegal	8.8	9.5	7.7	8.8	9.1	11.2	9.0	–2.2	10.8	11.9
Togo	11.5	17.6	13.0	12.8	2.4	9.3	8.7	–0.7	11.5	12.6
CAEMC	13.0	13.4	14.2	12.1	12.2	14.0	16.0	2.0	16.8	17.6
Cameroon	11.1	11.8	11.8	10.6	10.2	9.9	14.1	4.3	16.0	17.5
Central African Republic	6.0	7.1	5.8	5.7	5.5	6.5	6.4	–0.1	6.6	6.9
Chad	0.5	0.5	0.4	0.5	0.8	1.0	1.0	—	1.4	2.4
Congo	14.8	14.0	18.0	15.0	12.2	25.5	18.7	–6.8	18.1	17.3
Equatorial Guinea	14.7	9.2	26.6	8.1	14.9	12.1	34.8	22.7	22.8	12.4
Gabon	20.4	21.3	22.0	18.3	19.8	20.8	23.2	2.4	23.8	24.3
Zone	10.5	10.8	11.2	10.2	9.7	12.0	12.4	0.4	13.0	14.0
Comoros	10.1	14.9	8.8	9.8	6.9	10.3	11.8	1.5	11.9	12.7

Sources: Data provided by the authorities; and Fund staff estimates and projections as of the end of May 1995.

Table 12. Gross Domestic Savings, 1990–96
(In percent of GDP)

	1990–93 Average	1990	1991	1992	1993	1994 Original program	1994 Provi-sional	1994 Deviation	1995 Program/ Projections	1996 Projections
WAEMU	9.3	10.1	10.2	9.5	7.6	13.5	14.0	0.5	15.8	16.7
Benin	5.2	5.5	6.0	4.4	4.9	6.4	9.5	3.1	9.4	10.8
Burkina Faso	5.9	8.3	4.6	4.9	5.6	6.8	6.1	–0.7	6.0	7.3
Côte d'Ivoire	14.9	14.3	16.2	16.4	12.8	26.6	26.8	0.2	28.1	27.5
Mali	6.4	6.2	7.1	5.2	7.1	3.9	5.4	1.6	9.1	10.2
Niger	3.6	4.0	7.5	1.8	1.3	1.0	0.7	–0.3	1.8	3.8
Senegal	7.3	8.7	6.7	7.6	6.2	9.1	8.4	–0.7	11.3	13.1
Togo	6.6	13.1	9.5	7.1	–3.2	2.7	7.1	4.4	11.8	15.2
CAEMC	19.7	20.6	20.5	18.2	19.3	24.9	29.9	5.0	29.4	30.2
Cameroon	15.7	16.2	16.5	14.3	15.7	17.3	22.9	5.6	24.6	26.1
Central African Republic	2.0	1.1	3.1	0.1	3.7	6.0	7.7	1.7	7.0	8.1
Chad	–9.4	–4.0	–11.1	–11.1	–11.5	–9.8	–2.6	7.2	–3.2	–4.9
Congo	17.8	21.6	18.6	20.9	10.0	27.0	27.3	0.3	25.6	32.1
Equatorial Guinea	10.1	10.8	14.7	2.9	12.0	22.3	24.1	1.7	19.2	22.7
Gabon	40.0	40.8	41.4	37.0	40.7	48.5	56.3	7.8	53.9	52.3
Zone	14.0	15.0	14.9	13.4	12.8	18.3	21.0	2.7	21.7	22.6
Comoros	–1.8	–5.4	–3.7	0.6	1.1	–1.5	4.4	5.9	3.9	5.8

Sources: Data provided by the authorities; and Fund staff estimates and projections as of the end of May 1995.

Table 13. Government Domestic Savings, 1990–96
(In percent of GDP)

	1990–93 Average	1990	1991	1992	1993	1994 Original program	1994 Provi-sional	1994 Deviation	1995 Program/ Projections	1996 Projections
WAEMU	1.0	1.0	1.9	1.1	–0.1	2.1	2.2	0.0	3.7	4.8
Benin	–1.4	–2.9	–1.0	–2.8	1.1	0.6	0.9	0.3	1.1	2.0
Burkina Faso	3.3	2.9	4.2	2.9	3.0	–4.2	2.5	6.7	2.9	3.9
Côte d'Ivoire	0.8	0.8	1.4	1.8	–0.7	5.7	5.9	0.2	6.8	7.4
Mali	1.5	3.7	1.5	—	1.0	1.2	1.5	0.3	2.1	3.7
Niger	–0.8	0.4	–0.2	–2.1	–1.5	0.3	–3.4	–3.7	–1.3	0.8
Senegal	2.7	0.7	5.2	3.0	1.8	4.0	1.6	–2.4	4.6	5.8
Togo	–3.9	1.2	–3.0	–1.8	–12.1	–11.7	–10.0	1.7	–3.9	–1.4
CAEMC	–1.3	–0.1	–0.8	–1.7	–2.8	0.1	–0.3	–0.4	3.5	5.2
Cameroon	–3.2	–2.4	–2.8	–3.3	–4.5	–4.5	–5.9	–1.4	–0.5	1.7
Central African Republic	–6.2	–3.8	–8.5	–6.7	–5.9	–2.5	–5.3	–2.8	–2.2	–0.9
Chad	–6.0	–5.0	–6.3	–6.0	–6.6	–5.1	–6.1	–1.0	–3.0	–2.6
Congo	–2.1	7.5	–2.5	–4.5	–8.9	3.5	4.6	1.1	5.6	10.0
Equatorial Guinea	–10.1	–15.6	–12.8	–7.6	–4.3	–5.5	6.0	11.5	–2.3	–0.7
Gabon	5.5	3.7	7.8	5.5	4.9	8.0	10.3	2.3	13.9	13.8
Zone	–0.1	0.5	0.7	–0.2	–1.3	1.3	1.0	–0.3	3.6	5.0
Comoros	–8.5	–8.9	–11.3	–6.5	–7.2	–6.9	–10.6	–3.7	–5.8	–3.6

Sources: Data provided by the authorities; and Fund staff estimates and projections as of the end of May 1995.
Note: Excluding interest payments on debt service and official grants.

Table 14. Private Domestic Savings, 1990–96
(In percent of GDP)

	1990–93 Average	1990	1991	1992	1993	1994 Original program	1994 Provi-sional	1994 Deviation	1995 Program/ Projections	1996 Projections
WAEMU	8.4	9.1	8.3	8.4	7.7	11.4	11.9	0.5	12.1	11.9
Benin	6.6	8.4	7.0	7.2	3.7	5.9	8.7	2.8	8.3	8.8
Burkina Faso	2.6	5.4	0.4	2.0	2.7	11.0	3.7	–7.3	3.0	3.4
Côte d'Ivoire	14.1	13.5	14.8	14.6	13.5	20.9	20.9	—	21.3	20.1
Mali	4.8	2.5	5.5	5.2	6.2	2.7	4.0	1.3	7.0	6.6
Niger	4.5	3.6	7.7	3.9	2.8	0.7	4.1	3.4	3.1	3.0
Senegal	4.6	8.0	1.5	4.6	4.4	5.1	6.7	1.6	6.7	7.3
Togo	10.5	11.8	12.5	8.8	8.9	14.4	17.1	2.7	15.7	16.6
CAEMC	21.0	20.7	21.2	19.9	22.1	24.8	30.2	5.4	25.9	25.0
Cameroon	18.9	18.6	19.3	17.6	20.2	21.8	28.8	7.1	25.1	24.3
Central African Republic	8.2	4.8	11.6	6.8	9.6	8.5	13.0	4.5	9.2	9.1
Chad	–3.4	1.0	–4.8	–5.1	–4.9	–4.7	3.5	8.2	–0.2	–2.3
Congo	19.9	14.1	21.1	25.4	18.9	23.5	22.7	–0.8	20.0	22.1
Equatorial Guinea	20.1	26.4	27.4	10.5	16.3	27.8	18.0	–9.7	21.6	23.4
Gabon	34.5	37.1	33.6	31.5	35.8	40.5	46.0	5.5	40.0	38.5
Zone	14.1	14.5	14.2	13.6	14.1	17.0	20.0	3.0	18.1	17.6
Comoros	6.6	3.5	7.6	7.1	8.3	5.4	15.0	9.6	9.7	9.4

Sources: Data provided by the authorities; and Fund staff estimates and projections as of the end of May 1995.

Table 15. Gross National Savings, 1990–96
(In percent of GDP)

	1990–93 Average	1990	1991	1992	1993	1994 Original program	1994 Provi-sional	1994 Deviation	1995 Program/ Projections	1996 Projections
WAEMU	5.2	4.3	6.5	5.9	4.1	9.8	10.1	0.2	11.4	12.5
Benin	8.7	9.8	9.8	6.9	8.6	9.2	12.4	3.1	10.9	12.2
Burkina Faso	19.7	20.2	17.6	20.9	20.4	26.5	22.6	–3.9	20.1	18.6
Côte d'Ivoire	–0.6	–3.9	1.6	1.6	–1.6	11.7	11.7	—	12.8	13.5
Mali	8.1	7.7	9.1	6.9	8.7	6.5	7.5	1.0	11.5	12.8
Niger	5.2	3.7	8.6	3.5	4.8	2.8	5.4	2.6	3.6	4.2
Senegal	3.8	3.8	4.1	4.3	2.9	5.2	4.5	–0.7	7.9	9.8
Togo	10.4	18.8	14.1	10.8	–2.1	1.4	5.5	4.1	11.9	16.4
CAEMC	13.2	15.3	14.7	11.3	11.5	11.0	17.8	6.7	18.1	19.4
Cameroon	10.8	12.4	12.5	9.3	9.1	5.0	13.4	8.4	15.6	18.0
Central African Republic	8.0	5.5	9.9	7.7	9.0	7.1	11.7	4.6	12.2	12.8
Chad	3.8	10.8	2.5	1.9	0.1	2.9	10.1	7.3	9.9	7.1
Congo	4.0	10.3	2.0	4.9	–1.4	8.4	1.0	–7.4	1.0	5.5
Equatorial Guinea	31.0	38.9	37.5	26.2	21.4	35.2	30.4	–4.8	33.2	33.8
Gabon	25.8	27.2	29.1	21.6	25.1	23.7	35.9	12.2	33.2	32.7
Zone	8.8	9.4	10.3	8.3	7.4	10.3	13.5	3.1	14.3	15.5
Comoros	16.1	18.5	13.9	14.5	17.6	15.0	19.9	4.9	15.0	16.1

Sources: Data provided by the authorities; and Fund staff estimates and projections as of the end of May 1995.

Table 16. Resource Balance, 1990–96
(In percent of GDP)

	1990–93 Average	1990	1991	1992	1993	1994 Original program	1994 Provi-sional	1994 Deviation	1995 Program/ Projections	1996 Projections
WAEMU	–4.1	–3.4	–3.6	–4.4	–5.0	–4.4	–1.7	2.7	–1.0	–1.4
Benin	–9.2	–8.7	–8.5	–9.5	–10.0	–15.0	–4.7	10.2	–5.9	–5.8
Burkina Faso	–15.8	–12.1	–16.3	–16.7	–18.0	–25.1	–19.1	6.0	–17.8	–17.1
Côte d'Ivoire	5.3	5.6	5.7	5.6	4.2	12.5	12.7	0.2	13.0	11.0
Mali	–16.0	–16.2	–16.1	–16.7	–14.8	–23.0	–21.1	2.0	–16.9	–16.3
Niger	–3.5	–4.1	–1.7	–3.7	–4.4	–11.1	–7.6	3.5	–8.3	–7.6
Senegal	–5.9	–4.9	–5.6	–6.4	–7.0	–6.8	–5.3	1.5	–4.3	–4.0
Togo	–9.1	–11.8	–8.0	–9.2	–7.1	–9.8	–3.8	6.0	–3.5	–1.9
CAEMC	2.2	1.9	2.0	2.0	2.7	5.3	10.4	5.1	8.5	8.3
Cameroon	0.2	–1.2	0.5	—	1.6	4.1	7.1	3.0	6.5	6.2
Central African Republic	–11.2	–13.1	–10.3	–13.0	–8.5	–9.1	–6.2	2.9	–8.0	–7.0
Chad	–20.8	–22.6	–19.0	–19.5	–22.1	–24.7	–17.0	7.7	–17.0	–19.4
Congo	1.5	4.9	–0.3	5.2	–3.9	–6.5	5.5	12.0	4.7	9.9
Equatorial Guinea	–21.0	–15.8	–28.5	–21.4	–18.3	–1.6	–17.9	–16.3	–13.3	1.6
Gabon	15.6	17.0	14.9	14.2	16.2	22.1	29.3	7.2	24.7	22.5
Zone	–1.3	–1.0	–1.0	–1.5	–1.6	–0.4	3.6	4.0	3.2	2.8
Comoros	–19.2	–25.6	–18.2	–19.5	–13.5	–21.9	–16.8	5.0	–15.1	–13.8

Sources: Data provided by the authorities; and Fund staff estimates and projections as of the end of May 1995.

Table 17. Exports Value (f.o.b.), 1991–96
(Annual percentage changes)

	1991–93 Average	1991	1992	1993	1994 Original program	1994 Provi-sional	1994 Deviation	1995 Program/ Projections	1996 Projections
WAEMU[1]	–3.3	–2.3	–3.9	–3.6	120.8	109.3	–11.5	13.8	8.2
Benin	7.7	21.5	3.5	–1.7	101.1	73.0	–28.2	18.6	7.8
Burkina Faso	–3.5	–8.7	4.5	–6.2	140.0	103.8	–36.2	13.9	3.8
Côte d'Ivoire	–3.3	–6.3	–1.9	–1.6	127.3	115.4	–11.9	14.2	8.0
Mali	2.1	9.1	–11.5	8.7	111.6	97.1	–14.5	17.4	5.5
Niger	–6.6	–2.8	–7.1	–9.9	89.2	91.1	1.9	1.2	7.0
Senegal	–5.8	–4.4	–5.7	–7.2	117.7	116.6	–1.1	8.7	8.0
Togo	–15.6	3.1	–22.0	–28.0	94.1	97.4	3.4	23.6	21.1
CAEMC[1]	–3.0	–8.0	–6.0	4.9	81.0	106.3	25.4	3.0	9.4
Cameroon	–3.8	–4.0	–11.1	3.7	88.7	127.4	38.7	4.5	5.1
Central African Republic	–1.6	–13.7	–13.3	22.1	138.7	127.5	–11.2	8.0	14.5
Chad	–6.3	3.6	–11.7	–10.8	97.0	94.0	–3.0	39.4	14.9
Congo	–5.9	–17.3	–0.2	–0.3	64.8	81.1	16.3	–5.2	29.4
Equatorial Guinea	16.8	–2.0	37.0	15.3	161.4	100.6	–60.8	16.4	7.9
Gabon	–1.5	–7.6	–5.0	8.2	73.2	98.3	25.1	1.1	1.2
Zone[1]	–3.1	–5.3	–5.0	1.0	101.3	107.7	6.4	8.3	8.8
Comoros	11.1	43.8	–17.4	7.0	31.1	–24.6	–55.7	47.8	–1.5

Sources: Data provided by the authorities; and Fund staff estimates and projections as of the end of May 1995.

[1]Unadjusted for intra–CFA franc zone/subzone trade and reexports. Weighted average using the corresponding exports value (f.o.b.) of the respective countries.

Table 18. Exports—Volume, 1991–96
(Annual percentage changes)

	1991–93 Average	1991	1992	1993	1994 Original program	1994 Provi-sional	1994 Deviation	1995 Program/ Projections	1996 Projections
WAEMU[1]	–0.3	3.7	–1.3	–3.5	4.4	4.7	0.3	7.3	8.5
Benin	15.6	44.5	4.3	–1.9	2.2	3.0	0.8	11.3	28.3
Burkina Faso	–0.2	–6.2	4.5	1.1	9.0	–0.7	–9.7	8.7	5.4
Côte d'Ivoire	–3.0	–5.3	0.9	–4.6	2.0	3.7	1.7	4.9	6.8
Mali	7.1	11.9	1.6	7.8	4.3	0.6	–3.7	13.9	9.6
Niger	–0.4	0.2	2.5	–4.0	0.6	5.5	4.9	2.4	2.5
Senegal	–2.4	7.6	–8.2	–6.5	6.8	8.6	1.8	7.2	7.5
Togo	–9.2	5.9	–17.1	–16.4	11.6	16.1	4.5	10.7	5.7
CAEMC[1]	0.2	–4.6	3.2	1.9	1.0	5.8	4.8	1.3	7.1
Cameroon	–1.8	–3.7	2.8	–4.4	–3.0	5.9	8.9	–0.8	5.3
Central African Republic	2.5	–3.2	–10.0	20.7	19.5	11.0	–8.5	0.5	15.2
Chad	–2.1	1.1	–2.9	–4.4	6.3	–3.8	–10.1	28.2	14.3
Congo	–2.5	–17.1	9.8	–0.3	0.7	–1.6	–2.3	–2.4	19.3
Equatorial Guinea	33.5	–9.7	79.9	30.2	22.3	3.0	–19.3	21.2	13.6
Gabon	4.2	–1.5	2.9	11.1	1.3	9.9	8.6	0.7	1.4
Zone[1]	–0.2	–0.1	0.7	–1.1	3.0	5.2	2.2	4.7	7.9
Comoros	18.7	53.2	–17.6	20.4	–9.0	–35.8	–26.8	41.3	–3.2

Sources: Data provided by the authorities; and Fund staff estimates and projections as of the end of May 1995.
[1]Unadjusted for intra–CFA franc zone/subzone trade and reexports. Weighted average using the corresponding exports value (f.o.b.) of the respective countries.

Table 19. Imports Value (f.o.b.), 1991–96
(Annual percentage changes)

	1991–93 Average	1991	1992	1993	1994 Original program	1994 Provi-sional	1994 Deviation	1995 Program/ Projections	1996 Projections
WAEMU[1]	–0.8	1.5	0.8	–4.7	105.5	75.6	–29.9	12.4	11.2
Benin	9.6	16.8	9.0	2.8	97.4	33.2	–64.2	18.8	8.5
Burkina Faso	3.8	2.9	5.2	3.3	109.0	56.3	–52.7	10.7	5.6
Côte d'Ivoire	0.1	3.9	2.2	–5.9	108.4	83.0	–25.5	15.6	17.6
Mali	2.8	7.2	1.5	–0.3	105.1	91.9	–13.2	4.6	7.1
Niger	–17.3	–18.6	–11.9	–21.3	127.2	88.3	–38.9	11.4	5.6
Senegal	–0.5	–0.9	1.0	–1.8	98.6	82.8	–15.8	6.3	5.9
Togo	–19.2	–8.3	–15.1	–34.3	92.5	62.3	–30.2	22.1	12.6
CAEMC[1]	–3.0	–2.9	–10.4	4.4	86.0	77.9	–8.1	9.5	10.0
Cameroon	–8.4	–14.9	–13.8	3.5	57.5	87.3	29.8	3.5	6.9
Central African Republic	–11.5	–23.4	–0.8	–10.4	96.4	69.9	–26.6	23.4	7.8
Chad	–6.2	–0.1	–8.8	–9.6	89.8	64.7	–25.1	36.8	13.1
Congo	1.7	–0.1	–16.8	22.1	130.9	68.8	–62.0	5.2	24.4
Equatorial Guinea	13.6	80.5	–35.3	–4.5	91.3	117.5	26.2	4.0	–24.6
Gabon	3.1	10.8	–3.4	2.0	84.2	70.4	–13.9	10.4	6.1
Zone[1]	–1.6	–0.2	–3.3	–1.2	98.6	76.5	–22.1	11.3	10.8
Comoros	4.9	13.0	10.8	–9.1	52.9	32.9	–20.0	8.6	4.0

Sources: Data provided by the authorities; and Fund staff estimates and projections as of the end of May 1995.
[1]Unadjusted for intra–CFA franc zone/subzone trade and imports for reexports. Weighted average using the corresponding imports value (f.o.b.) of the respective countries.

Table 20. Imports—Volume, 1991–96
(Annual percentage changes)

	1991–93 Average	1991	1992	1993	1994 Original program	1994 Provi-sional	1994 Deviation	1995 Program/ Projections	1996 Projections
WAEMU[1]	–0.4	0.8	3.9	–5.8	–1.0	–9.9	–8.8	13.5	9.1
Benin	8.9	17.8	8.5	0.4	–6.5	–33.0	–26.5	23.7	10.6
Burkina Faso	4.8	2.8	9.6	1.9	–2.1	–13.9	–11.8	10.9	3.6
Côte d'Ivoire	0.5	2.6	7.0	–8.0	2.3	–6.8	–9.1	17.9	14.5
Mali	–0.2	–0.9	2.2	–1.9	–0.9	–4.8	–3.9	6.5	4.1
Niger	–10.7	–19.2	–9.4	–3.6	5.2	–9.1	–14.3	13.3	3.5
Senegal	–0.2	1.0	3.0	–4.7	–3.0	–4.4	–1.4	5.2	4.2
Togo	–18.6	–10.0	–10.5	–35.2	–8.6	–19.9	–11.3	17.3	10.6
CAEMC[1]	0.9	0.9	–2.4	4.1	–7.2	–12.0	–4.8	11.2	6.7
Cameroon	0.3	–2.5	–0.2	3.5	–16.7	–3.9	12.8	7.5	—
Central African Republic	–9.6	–25.1	3.4	–7.1	–19.3	–11.9	7.4	21.9	4.9
Chad	–6.9	–3.0	–7.1	–10.5	–5.8	–18.8	–13.0	27.6	21.3
Congo	1.7	–1.9	–13.7	20.8	12.3	–23.9	–36.2	15.1	19.9
Equatorial Guinea	12.4	66.8	–27.3	–2.4	–5.6	17.4	23.0	8.7	–20.5
Gabon	3.9	8.9	1.6	1.1	–8.0	–18.2	–10.2	7.5	5.0
Zone[1]	0.2	0.8	1.6	–2.0	–3.2	–10.7	–7.5	12.6	8.2
Comoros	4.7	8.2	14.4	–8.5	–3.9	–10.2	–6.3	2.4	2.6

Sources: Data provided by the authorities; and Fund staff estimates and projections as of the end of May 1995.
[1]Unadjusted for intra–CFA franc zone/subzone trade and imports for reexports. Weighted average using the corresponding imports value (f.o.b.) of the respective countries.

Table 21. Trade Balance, 1990–96
(In percent of GDP)

	1990–93 Average	1990	1991	1992	1993	1994 Original program	1994 Provi-sional	1994 Deviation	1995 Program/ Projections	1996 Projections
WAEMU[1]	0.4	1.4	0.6	–0.3	—	2.0	4.6	2.6	4.8	4.2
Benin	–8.3	–7.6	–7.7	–8.8	–9.3	–13.7	–4.3	9.4	–4.2	–4.4
Burkina Faso	–10.0	–8.6	–9.7	–10.2	–11.4	–15.9	–10.3	5.5	–9.6	–9.4
Côte d'Ivoire	10.9	13.1	10.6	9.7	10.4	19.1	19.8	0.8	19.5	17.3
Mali	–1.0	–0.6	–0.4	–2.1	–1.0	–1.3	–0.9	0.4	1.2	1.0
Niger	–2.8	–5.9	–3.0	–2.0	–0.3	–3.4	–0.1	3.3	–1.5	–1.3
Senegal	–5.7	–4.7	–5.3	–6.1	–6.8	–7.8	–6.0	1.8	–5.2	–4.8
Togo	–4.6	–7.1	–3.7	–4.9	–2.7	–3.1	1.4	4.5	1.7	3.3
CAEMC[1]	11.7	12.3	10.9	11.2	12.3	17.5	21.0	3.5	18.3	18.0
Cameroon	5.0	3.7	5.3	5.1	5.7	12.4	12.7	0.3	11.6	11.0
Central African Republic	–4.4	–6.3	–4.0	–5.3	–2.1	0.3	1.9	1.6	–0.3	0.7
Chad	–5.0	–5.6	–4.6	–4.6	–5.0	–5.7	–2.7	2.9	–2.9	–2.6
Congo	25.3	31.2	22.5	25.3	22.3	23.9	34.6	10.7	29.8	33.9
Equatorial Guinea	–14.9	–10.8	–42.1	–6.7	—	16.5	–4.0	–20.5	1.8	16.0
Gabon	27.0	31.2	25.3	24.7	26.9	32.3	41.2	8.9	37.1	34.8
Zone[1]	5.5	6.4	5.3	4.9	5.4	8.5	11.9	3.4	10.7	10.2
Comoros	–11.7	–11.3	–10.2	–14.0	–11.1	–16.9	–15.9	0.9	–14.3	–14.3

Sources: Data provided by the authorities; and Fund staff estimates and projections as of the end of May 1995.
[1] Unadjusted for intra–CFA franc zone/subzone trade.

Table 22. Intra-CFA Franc Zone Trade, in 1990–93 and 1994
(In percent of total trade)

	Exports		Imports	
	1990–93	1994	1990–93	1994
WAEMU				
Benin	8.0	2.8	5.5	3.6
Burkina Faso	8.5	14.9	24.5	31.2
Côte d'Ivoire	17.6	17.6	1.7	1.7
Mali	3.6	2.4	26.7	22.9
Niger	3.3	9.2	10.3	12.9
Senegal	14.0	19.4	9.8	9.7
Togo	6.9	6.4	8.8	11.7
CAEMC				
Cameroon	9.5	16.3	3.5	8.2
Central African Republic	0.3	0.6	6.5	4.7
Chad	0.5	0.4	13.2	29.0
Congo	—	0.1	4.7	5.6
Equatorial Guinea	—	—	36.9	37.6
Gabon	1.2	1.0	11.7	19.9
Comoros	—	—	—	—

Source: IMF, *Direction of Trade Statistics Yearbook*.

Table 23. External Current Account, Excluding Official Transfers, 1990–96
(In percent of GDP)

	1990–93 Average	1990	1991	1992	1993	1994 Original program	1994 Provi-sional	1994 Deviation	1995 Program/ Projections	1996 Projections
WAEMU	−10.7	−11.7	−10.1	−10.2	−10.8	−13.0	−8.0	5.0	−6.6	−6.7
Benin	−6.8	−6.2	−5.7	−8.0	−7.5	−14.4	−3.1	11.2	−5.4	−5.3
Burkina Faso	−11.9	−8.5	−13.2	−12.1	−13.9	−21.5	−13.9	7.6	−13.0	−12.6
Côte d'Ivoire	−11.5	−14.0	−10.5	−10.0	−11.5	−8.6	−2.7	5.9	−2.9	−3.7
Mali	−14.2	−14.8	−14.0	−15.0	−13.2	−20.4	−19.0	1.4	−14.5	−13.7
Niger	−8.3	−11.8	−7.4	−6.7	−7.4	−16.1	−12.6	3.5	−12.8	−11.9
Senegal	−9.5	−9.1	−9.1	−9.6	−10.2	−11.0	−9.2	1.9	−7.7	−7.3
Togo	−10.2	−13.1	−9.0	−10.4	−8.4	−13.7	−8.2	5.6	6.4	4.1
CAEMC	−7.3	−6.9	−7.1	−7.8	−7.5	−11.5	−4.1	7.4	−5.0	−4.6
Cameroon	−6.5	−6.9	−5.9	−6.8	−6.1	−9.5	−3.6	5.9	−3.4	−2.6
Central African Republic	−14.8	−16.8	−13.7	−15.9	−12.9	−15.1	−12.8	2.3	−12.7	−11.8
Chad	−23.6	−25.1	−20.8	−21.9	−26.5	−29.5	−19.2	10.3	−18.4	−21.1
Congo	−14.8	−11.3	−18.9	−12.3	−16.8	−28.2	−21.4	6.8	−21.2	−17.4
Equatorial Guinea	−42.1	−45.0	−65.8	−31.0	−26.9	−10.2	−26.3	−16.1	−20.2	−3.1
Gabon	1.1	3.0	2.5	−1.4	0.3	−3.2	8.4	11.6	3.6	2.5
Zone	−9.1	−9.1	−9.4	−8.8	−9.1	−12.3	−6.3	6.1	−5.9	−5.8
Comoros	−18.3	−21.5	−17.3	−20.8	−13.7	−20.1	−16.5	3.6	−14.3	−13.4

Sources: Data provided by the authorities; and Fund staff estimates and projections as of the end of May 1995.

Table 24. External Current Account, Including Official Transfers, 1990–96

(In percent of GDP)

	1990–93 Average	1990	1991	1992	1993	1994 Original program	1994 Provi-sional	1994 Deviation	1995 Program/ Projections	1996 Projections
WAEMU	–5.8	–6.7	–4.9	–5.4	–6.0	–6.8	–2.1	4.7	–2.8	–3.1
Benin	–0.5	1.0	–0.4	–1.8	–0.7	–4.6	2.4	6.9	0.5	–0.2
Burkina Faso	–1.9	–0.3	–3.4	–0.7	–3.3	–5.4	–2.7	2.6	–3.7	–5.8
Côte d'Ivoire	–10.3	–12.6	–9.1	–9.4	–10.0	–7.7	–2.4	5.3	–2.2	–2.9
Mali	–4.0	–5.6	–1.7	–4.0	–4.7	–8.0	–4.4	3.6	–5.1	–4.7
Niger	–1.9	–4.4	–0.7	–1.9	–0.9	–9.3	–5.8	3.4	–8.5	–7.4
Senegal	–4.4	–3.8	–3.7	–4.5	–5.4	–4.4	0.2	4.6	–1.4	–1.5
Togo	–5.3	–6.1	–3.4	–5.5	–6.1	–11.1	–5.3	5.7	–3.5	–0.7
CAEMC	–4.4	–3.9	–3.9	–4.9	–5.0	–7.9	–1.7	6.2	–2.7	–2.5
Cameroon	–4.6	–5.1	–3.5	–5.0	–4.9	–6.8	–2.4	4.4	–2.5	–1.8
Central African Republic	–5.2	–8.7	–3.5	–5.4	–3.3	–6.7	–2.3	4.4	–2.8	–2.4
Chad	–7.5	–7.7	–5.3	–6.4	–10.5	–12.0	–4.2	7.8	–3.8	–7.4
Congo	–12.9	–9.0	–16.4	–10.8	–15.2	–25.1	–20.9	4.2	–19.6	–16.4
Equatorial Guinea	–11.5	–9.4	–34.5	2.1	–4.3	11.2	–11.6	–22.8	–0.7	12.7
Gabon	1.4	3.4	2.7	–1.2	0.6	–2.7	8.9	11.6	4.0	2.9
Zone	–5.2	–5.4	–4.4	–5.2	–5.6	–7.3	–1.9	5.3	–2.8	–2.9
Comoros	–1.6	–3.2	–0.6	–5.5	3.0	–5.4	–1.4	4.0	–4.0	–3.4

Sources: Data provided by the authorities; and Fund staff estimates and projections as of the end of May 1995.

Table 25. Terms of Trade, 1990–96

(Annual percentage changes)

	1990–93 Average	1990	1991	1992	1993	1994 Original program	1994 Provi-sional	1994 Deviation	1995 Program/ Projections	1996 Projections
WAEMU[1]	–2.6	–2.7	–2.6	–2.2	–2.8	–1.1	3.2	4.3	8.2	–1.9
Benin	1.6	40.5	–15.3	–17.7	–1.2	–8.2	3.3	11.5	27.3	–13.6
Burkina Faso	1.2	–8.7	18.6	4.2	–9.3	8.0	12.8	4.8	5.1	–3.5
Côte d'Ivoire	–2.8	–9.4	–1.0	—	–0.8	1.1	5.8	4.7	11.1	–1.6
Mali	–4.5	4.9	–9.8	–12.2	–0.9	–2.0	–2.9	–0.9	5.0	–6.4
Niger	–4.5	–9.8	–1.8	–4.9	–1.6	–13.6	–12.4	1.2	2.1	2.4
Senegal	–3.4	–4.5	–9.0	2.8	–2.8	—	5.1	5.1	–1.1	–1.6
Togo	–3.5	4.1	–2.9	–4.3	–10.9	–6.7	–3.9	2.8	13.6	17.1
CAEMC[1]	–0.1	6.3	–6.2	–3.7	3.0	–4.8	0.8	5.6	5.4	–3.6
Cameroon	–0.3	3.8	–6.6	–7.0	8.7	1.7	10.0	8.3	9.1	–7.2
Central African Republic	–1.6	–3.0	–12.7	2.8	6.6	–9.0	3.3	12.3	19.4	–2.8
Chad	–5.3	–5.9	0.1	–6.4	–8.9	0.7	0.2	–0.5	4.9	–1.5
Congo	2.7	9.6	–2.1	5.6	–2.2	–22.7	–8.6	14.1	–2.2	6.9
Equatorial Guinea	4.9	2.0	8.9	11.5	–2.8	5.6	5.7	0.1	0.3	—
Gabon	0.3	15.4	–7.8	–2.9	–3.5	–8.7	–13.3	–4.6	–2.2	–1.4
Zone[1]	–1.5	1.4	–4.3	–2.8	–0.2	–2.6	2.1	4.8	7.0	–2.6
Comoros	–5.2	–2.7	–10.9	3.3	–10.4	–8.7	–17.9	–9.2	–4.2	0.7

Sources: Data provided by the authorities; and Fund staff estimates and projections as of the end of May 1995.

[1] Average weighted by individual country GDP.

Table 26. Nominal and Real Effective Exchange Rates, 1991–94
(Percentage changes)

	Nominal Effective Exchange Rates					Real Effective Exchange Rates[1]				
	1991	1992	1993	Average 91–93	1994[2]	1991	1992	1993	Average 91–93	1994[2]
WAEMU[3]	3.2	8.7	6.8	6.2	–45.6	–4.6	0.8	–2.6	–2.1	–32.4
Benin	2.0	8.9	5.1	5.3	–49.5	–1.3	7.6	–2.0	1.5	–30.5
Burkina Faso	–1.3	1.6	–1.3	–0.3	–49.1	–2.8	–3.2	–3.2	–3.1	–35.8
Côte d'Ivoire	8.4	17.3	14.9	13.5	–40.5	–2.8	5.0	–2.3	—	–34.5
Mali	–1.1	1.4	1.2	0.5	–49.6	–3.5	–7.4	–2.1	–4.3	–35.0
Niger	–1.6	1.4	0.5	0.1	–49.3	–12.7	–6.0	–3.5	–7.4	–30.3
Senegal	0.8	3.5	2.0	2.1	–48.6	–6.9	–1.0	–2.4	–3.4	–30.2
Togo	3.8	9.7	7.7	7.1	–42.9	–4.6	2.8	–5.9	–2.6	–21.4
CAEMC[3]	3.5	8.7	6.7	6.3	–44.4	–1.0	–5.4	–6.3	–4.3	–26.2
Cameroon	3.6	9.1	7.0	6.6	–43.5	–3.5	–1.9	–7.1	–4.2	–25.7
Central African Republic	3.8	8.5	6.5	6.2	–43.7	–5.8	–0.2	–5.3	–3.7	–33.0
Chad	–2.0	0.9	1.4	0.1	–49.5	–3.0	–6.3	–8.9	–6.1	–27.4
Congo	–1.1	1.1	–0.6	–0.2	–49.5	3.9	0.6	–1.7	1.0	–19.8
Equatorial Guinea	2.7	10.2	16.0	9.6	–43.2	–8.8	–4.2	10.2	–0.9	–29.7
Gabon	6.2	12.8	10.0	9.7	–43.0	3.2	–15.7	–7.0	–6.5	–28.1
Zone[3]	3.3	8.7	6.7	6.3	–45.1	–3.0	–1.9	–4.3	–3.1	–29.7
Comoros	–0.1	4.8	1.2	2.0	–27.4					

Sources: Information Notice System (INS); and Fund staff estimates.
[1]Based on relative CPIs.
[2]Based on data for the fourth quarter.
[3]Weighted by 1994 nominal GDP.

Table 27. Stock of External Public Debt at End of 1994
(In percent of GDP)

	Official Creditors		Private Creditors	Short-Term Debt	Use of IMF Credit	Total	Of Which:	
	Bilateral	Multilateral[1]					Rescheduled debt[2]	Arrears[3]
WAEMU	50.8	49.1	24.9	0.4	5.0	130.3	26.4	26.9
Benin	31.1	50.9	—	1.0	3.8	86.7	15.9	—
Burkina Faso	30.5	52.8	—	—	2.5	85.8	8.5	1.1
Côte d'Ivoire	69.7	45.0	66.6	0.3	4.7	186.3	44.7	66.0
Mali	79.2	67.1	—	—	5.7	152.0	14.5	—
Niger	31.1	48.9	—	—	1.7	81.8	14.5	11.6
Senegal	29.1	40.2	2.2	1.3	7.4	80.2	13.4	2.1
Togo	51.8	69.3	—	—	8.4	129.5	44.3	21.2
CAEMC	77.3	27.6	13.6	1.6	1.6	121.8	48.0	13.9
Cameroon	73.6	23.8	10.3	3.3	0.6	111.6	35.0	12.9
Central African Republic	29.6	68.3	—	—	4.3	102.2	25.3	5.8
Chad	19.0	69.7	0.7	—	3.5	93.0	6.3	7.2
Congo	161.9	37.1	63.2	—	1.2	263.3	98.1	55.3
Equatorial Guinea	103.3	75.9	0.5	—	15.7	195.4	58.7	46.5
Gabon	70.0	11.2	4.8	—	2.2	88.1	64.7	—
Zone	62.5	39.6	19.9	1.0	3.5	126.5	36.0	21.1
Comoros	17.7	60.0	—	—	0.9	78.6	4.1	12.7

Sources: Data provided by the authorities; and Fund staff estimates as of the end of May 1995.
[1]Excluding IMF.
[2]Debt already rescheduled.
[3]Outstanding at end of 1994.

Table 28. Recent Paris Club Debt Reschedulings for the CFA Franc Countries

Country[1]	Date of Agreement	Amount Consolidated (In millions of U.S. dollars)	Consolidation Period: Start date	Consolidation Period: End date	Consolidation Period: Length (Months)	Fund Arrangement (Period)	Type of Debt Consolidated[2]: Current Maturities	Type of Debt Consolidated[2]: Previously rescheduled debt	Terms[3]	Goodwill Clause[4]	Comments[5]
Benin III	06/21/93	25	08/01/93	12/31/95	29	ESAF (1993–96)	PI	I	Enhanced concessions	Stock	Enhanced PRD excluded; Toronto PRD on LMIC terms
Burkina Faso II	05/07/93	36	04/01/93	12/31/95	33	ESAF (1993–96)	PIAL	—	Enhanced concessions	Yes/Stock	Toronto PRD excluded
Cameroon III	03/25/94	1,259	04/01/94	09/30/95	18	SBA (1994–95)	PIAL	PIAL	Enhanced concessions	Yes/Stock	Arrears rescheduled on LMIC terms
Central African Republic VI	04/12/94	30	04/01/94	03/31/95	12	SBA (1994–95)	PIAL	PIAL	Enhanced concessions	Yes/Stock	Toronto PRD rescheduled standard terms
Chad I[6]	10/24/89	38	10/01/89	12/31/90	15	SAF III (1990)	PIAL	—	Toronto terms	No	Few creditors
Congo III	06/30/94	1,227	07/01/94	05/31/95	11	SBA (1994–95)	PIAL	PIAL	Standard LMIC	Yes	PCOD arrears deferred within consolidation period
Côte d'Ivoire V	03/23/94	1,849	03/01/94	03/31/97	37	ESAF (1994–97)	PIAL	PIAL	Enhanced concessions	Yes/Stock	PCOD arrears deferred within consolidation period
Equatorial Guinea IV	12/15/94	51	06/01/94	02/28/96	21	ESAF (1993–96)	PIA	PIA	Enhanced concessions	Stock	Terms of reference Trigger clause, 6/1/95
Gabon VI	04/15/94	1,360	04/01/94	03/31/95	12	SBA (1994–95)	PIAL	PIAL	Graduated LMIC	Yes	Excluded 1991 PRD. PCOD arrears deferred
Mali III	10/29/92	21	10/01/92	08/31/95	35	ESAF (1992–95)	PIA PIA	Partial	Enhanced concessions	Yes/Stock	PRD included only for short-term amounts
Niger VIII	03/04/94	160	01/01/94	03/31/95	15	SBA (1994–95)	PIAL	PIAL	Enhanced concessions	Yes/Stock	Toronto PRD standard terms
Senegal X	03/03/94	240	01/01/94	03/31/95	15	SBA (1994–95)	PIAL	PIAL	Enhanced concessions	Yes/Stock	Toronto PRD standard terms; PCOD arrears deferred within consolidation period
Togo X	02/23/95	246	01/31/95	09/30/97	32	ESAF (1994–97)	PIAL	PI	Enhanced concessions	Yes/Stock	Topping up to 67 percent NPV for arrears of Toronto PRD; current maturities of Toronto PRD reprofiled non-concessionally (23 years/6 years grace); Paris Club X arrears on amounts deferred graduated repayment (10 years/2 years grace).

Source: Agreed minutes of Paris Club debt reschedulings.

[1]The roman numeral indicates the rank number of the last Paris Club rescheduling obtained by the country.

[2]Refers to medium- and long-term debt; P = Principal; I = Interest; A = Arrears; L = Late Interest.

[3]Enhanced concessions (received by most low-income countries since 1991) include three options that have in common that the net present value of the debt service on commercial debt is reduced by 50 percent; and one option that provides for longer maturities but no reductions in the net present value.

[4]The goodwill clause provides for the possibility of a new (flow) rescheduling after the current consolidation period ("Yes") or for a consideration of the stock of debt after a period of three years ("Stock").

[5]PRD = Previously Rescheduled Debt; LMIC = Lower Middle-Income Countries; PCOD = pre-cutoff date.

[6]Chad is currently seeking rescheduling on a bilateral basis.

Table 29. Total Scheduled Public Debt Service, 1990–96

(In percent of exports of goods and nonfactor services)

	1990–93 Average	1990	1991	1992	1993	1994 Original program	1994 Provi-sional	1994 Deviation	1995 Program/ Projections	1996 Projections
WAEMU	39.3	40.1	39.2	39.4	38.6	32.6	32.7	0.1	29.9	25.7
Benin	21.9	19.8	14.1	35.0	18.6	18.4	20.1	1.7	17.9	16.9
Of which: bilateral	16.9	12.6	10.0	30.6	14.5	13.7	14.5	0.8	12.0	10.7
multilateral	4.6	6.4	3.9	4.2	4.0	4.4	5.1	0.7	5.4	5.7
IMF	0.3	0.8	0.1	0.2	0.1	0.3	0.4	0.1	0.6	0.6
Burkina Faso	17.2	15.6	14.4	17.0	21.8	20.2	18.2	–2.0	19.2	18.8
Of which: bilateral	...	...	...	...	...	...	7.1	...	8.2	7.6
multilateral	...	...	...	...	...	...	10.9	...	10.8	10.8
IMF	...	...	...	...	...	...	0.2	...	0.2	0.4
Côte d'Ivoire	52.2	54.9	54.0	51.0	49.0	38.2	37.5	–0.7	35.7	29.0
Of which: bilateral	34.7	40.1	35.2	32.5	31.2	19.7	19.8	0.1	20.8	14.8
multilateral	13.0	7.3	14.4	14.8	15.5	15.9	15.1	–0.8	12.6	13.0
IMF	3.5	4.4	3.7	3.7	2.2	2.5	2.5	—	2.3	1.2
Mali	40.9	42.6	36.6	44.1	40.2	38.3	40.5	2.2	32.6	29.9
Of which: bilateral	31.1	31.7	27.6	34.8	30.2	29.0	29.8	0.8	22.9	20.2
multilateral	6.4	5.3	5.8	6.9	7.5	6.7	8.0	1.3	6.6	6.6
IMF	3.4	5.6	3.1	2.4	2.5	2.6	2.7	0.1	1.6	1.7
Niger	35.8	37.3	36.3	30.9	38.7	43.0	42.3	–0.7	35.1	34.6
Of which: bilateral	...	...	...	...	...	19.8	23.9	4.1	18.1	15.9
multilateral	...	...	...	...	...	16.5	11.4	–5.1	11.4	11.3
IMF	3.8	4.0	3.7	3.5	3.8	4.5	4.6	0.1	4.1	4.4
Senegal	26.7	30.9	27.6	24.3	24.0	22.5	22.3	–0.2	20.1	19.3
Of which: bilateral	...	...	...	...	...	9.3	11.1	1.8	8.3	7.5
multilateral	...	...	...	...	...	6.8	6.3	–0.5	6.6	6.0
IMF	3.9	4.9	4.4	3.7	2.5	2.4	2.5	0.1	2.9	3.1
Togo	21.0	...	20.8	24.9	38.2	35.9	39.4	3.5	26.7	21.3
Of which: bilateral	14.2	...	14.9	15.7	26.1	19.7	20.7	1.0	12.1	10.0
multilateral	2.6	...	2.7	3.3	4.2	5.0	5.1	0.1	4.8	4.2
IMF	2.0	...	2.4	2.9	2.9	2.6	2.4	–0.2	3.4	2.9
CAEMC	28.7	22.7	29.0	33.2	29.8	37.3	28.5	–8.8	37.9	31.3
Cameroon	31.8	20.5	31.2	39.5	35.9	34.0	29.0	–5.0	38.6	32.2
Of which: bilateral	16.9	6.9	19.1	23.6	17.9	18.6	16.4	–2.2	21.4	21.4
multilateral	7.2	4.6	7.0	9.5	7.6	6.6	5.9	–0.7	7.8	7.9
IMF	1.5	0.6	0.5	1.6	3.5	0.8	0.7	–0.1	0.3	0.4
Central African Republic	23.4	22.6	22.1	25.9	23.0	26.8	22.6	–4.2	25.1	19.7
Of which: bilateral	9.3	—	11.3	14.4	11.5	14.6	12.9	–1.7	14.6	9.3
multilateral	7.0	—	8.2	9.8	9.7	8.2	6.8	–1.4	7.2	6.9
IMF	2.6	4.5	2.6	1.6	1.8	4.0	2.9	–1.1	3.4	3.4
Chad	10.3	7.7	8.2	11.2	13.9	14.1	13.8	–0.3	34.1	11.9
Of which: bilateral	4.8	2.8	5.1	5.6	5.8	6.0	5.9	–0.1	29.8	8.1
multilateral	5.3	4.9	3.2	5.6	7.4	8.1	8.0	–0.1	4.2	3.8
IMF	0.7	1.9	—	—	0.7	1.1	1.1	—	2.4	2.4
Congo	38.8	32.1	40.9	42.7	39.5	60.5	50.7	–9.8	62.3	49.9
Of which: bilateral	...	...	...	36.8	33.7	33.8	34.9	1.1	38.9	33.9
multilateral	...	...	...	5.0	5.2	6.4	5.9	–0.5	8.0	5.2
IMF	...	...	...	0.3	0.1	0.4	0.3	–0.1	0.4	0.2
Equatorial Guinea	45.3	41.4	54.6	44.8	40.6	36.9	35.9	–0.9	27.0	18.1
Of which: bilateral	34.8	23.3	44.5	37.0	34.3	28.9	28.4	–0.5	20.6	12.7
multilateral	8.3	12.1	8.4	7.1	5.7	4.6	5.2	0.6	5.0	3.9
IMF	2.2	6.0	1.7	0.6	0.6	1.5	2.0	0.5	1.5	1.4
Gabon	22.7	20.7	23.1	25.1	21.9	31.8	20.6	–11.2	29.5	24.8
Of which: bilateral	19.6	18.2	20.0	21.6	18.7	27.6	17.9	–9.7	25.4	22.3
multilateral	1.9	1.7	1.9	2.0	1.8	2.6	1.7	–0.9	2.1	2.0
IMF	1.2	0.7	1.2	1.5	1.4	1.5	1.0	–0.5	1.9	0.5
Zone	34.0	31.3	34.2	36.4	34.2	34.7	30.6	–4.1	33.8	28.4
Comoros	24.1	34.0	23.0	21.3	18.1	16.2	25.9	9.7	25.2	22.4
Of which: bilateral	9.2	14.4	10.1	6.3	6.0	3.6	10.9	7.3	7.6	6.6
multilateral	14.9	19.6	12.9	15.0	12.1	12.7	14.9	2.2	17.6	15.8
IMF	—	—	—	—	—	—	—	—	—	—

Sources: Data provided by the authorities; and Fund staff estimates and projections as of the end of May 1995.

Table 30. Total Scheduled External Public Debt Service, 1990–96
(In percent of total government revenue)

	1990–93 Average	1990	1991	1992	1993	1994 Original program	1994 Provi-sional	1994 Deviation	1995 Program/ Projections	1996 Projections
WAEMU	57.9	57.5	57.1	56.3	60.6	73.4	72.4	–1.1	63.3	53.1
Benin	43.5	43.5	29.6	68.3	32.4	47.3	42.7	–4.6	35.4	33.1
Of which: bilateral	33.4	27.7	21.1	59.7	25.2	35.1	30.9	–4.2	23.6	20.9
multilateral	9.4	14.0	8.3	8.2	6.9	11.3	10.9	–0.4	10.6	11.1
IMF	0.7	1.8	0.2	0.4	0.3	0.9	0.9	0.1	1.2	1.1
Burkina Faso	17.1	17.1	13.1	18.0	20.4	36.0	28.2	–7.8	30.5	26.9
Of which: bilateral	...	...	...	...	...	...	11.0	...	13.0	10.9
multilateral	...	...	...	...	...	...	16.9	...	17.2	15.5
IMF	...	...	...	...	...	...	0.3	...	0.2	0.6
Côte d'Ivoire	82.7	84.2	83.5	76.7	86.2	90.0	83.5	–6.5	80.5	65.9
Of which: bilateral	54.9	61.5	54.5	48.9	54.9	46.5	44.2	–2.3	47.0	33.6
multilateral	20.8	11.2	22.3	22.3	27.3	37.6	33.7	–3.8	28.4	29.6
IMF	5.5	6.8	5.8	5.6	4.0	5.9	5.6	–0.4	5.2	2.8
Mali	43.7	41.9	40.0	47.6	45.4	70.8	67.8	–3.0	55.1	46.4
Of which: bilateral	33.2	31.2	30.2	37.5	34.1	53.6	49.9	–0.8	38.8	31.4
multilateral	6.9	5.2	6.4	7.4	8.5	12.3	13.5	1.1	11.2	10.2
IMF	3.6	5.5	3.4	2.6	2.8	4.9	4.5	–0.4	2.8	2.7
Niger	63.9	61.6	72.8	53.3	67.8	85.5	116.6	31.1	72.1	56.7
Of which: bilateral	...	...	...	...	...	39.3	65.8	26.5	37.3	26.1
multilateral	...	...	...	...	...	32.8	31.5	–1.3	23.4	18.5
IMF	6.7	6.6	7.4	6.1	6.7	8.9	12.6	3.8	8.3	7.2
Senegal	35.1	40.6	34.5	31.2	34.2	48.6	56.7	8.1	44.3	42.0
Of which: bilateral	...	...	...	...	...	20.2	28.2	8.0	18.4	16.4
multilateral	...	...	...	...	...	14.7	16.0	1.3	14.5	13.1
IMF	5.1	6.4	5.6	4.8	3.6	5.3	6.3	1.1	6.5	6.8
Togo	55.4	...	39.9	41.3	85.1	104.1	99.4	–4.6	53.7	42.8
Of which: bilateral	...	...	28.5	26.2	58.1	57.1	52.3	–4.8	24.3	20.0
multilateral	...	...	5.2	5.5	9.5	14.4	13.0	–1.4	9.6	8.5
IMF	...	...	4.5	4.8	6.4	7.4	6.0	–1.4	6.7	5.9
CAEMC	49.8	41.0	47.2	52.7	58.1	81.5	85.6	4.1	88.2	69.3
Cameroon	44.2	28.7	41.6	46.8	59.7	71.6	100.7	29.0	85.6	64.7
Of which: bilateral	23.2	9.6	25.5	27.9	29.7	39.2	57.0	17.8	47.6	42.9
multilateral	9.9	6.5	9.3	11.3	12.7	13.9	20.6	6.7	17.3	15.8
IMF	2.3	0.8	0.6	1.9	5.8	1.8	2.5	0.7	0.6	0.9
Central African Republic	34.2	31.3	30.3	33.5	41.5	57.5	65.5	8.0	53.8	39.8
Of which: bilateral	13.7	—	15.4	18.7	20.8	31.3	37.3	6.0	31.3	18.9
multilateral	10.4	—	11.3	12.8	17.6	17.7	19.8	2.1	15.3	13.9
IMF	3.8	6.3	3.6	2.1	3.2	8.5	8.5	–0.1	7.2	6.8
Chad	19.5	15.5	16.1	19.7	26.5	33.3	51.1	17.7	107.2	36.2
Of which: bilateral	9.1	5.7	9.9	9.9	11.0	14.1	21.6	7.5	93.9	24.7
multilateral	10.0	9.8	6.2	9.9	14.1	19.2	29.4	10.2	13.3	11.4
IMF	1.3	3.8	—	—	1.4	2.5	3.9	1.4	7.4	7.4
Congo	77.9	63.7	72.7	81.4	93.7	148.5	133.7	–14.8	165.2	134.3
Of which: bilateral	...	...	...	70.3	79.8	83.1	92.1	9.0	103.3	91.3
multilateral	...	...	...	9.5	12.4	15.8	15.5	–0.3	21.1	14.0
IMF	...	...	1.0	0.6	0.2	1.0	0.8	–0.2	1.1	0.5
Equatorial Guinea	75.8	63.2	84.4	78.4	77.2	107.1	100.8	–6.2	80.7	50.3
Of which: bilateral	58.6	35.5	68.8	64.8	65.2	84.0	79.7	–4.3	61.5	35.5
multilateral	13.7	18.4	13.0	12.5	10.9	13.5	14.6	1.2	14.8	11.0
IMF	3.5	9.2	2.6	1.1	1.1	4.5	5.7	1.2	4.4	3.9
Gabon	47.6	48.7	44.9	51.1	45.9	67.1	57.4	–9.7	66.8	53.8
Of which: bilateral	41.2	43.0	38.9	43.8	39.2	58.3	49.9	–8.3	57.6	48.4
multilateral	3.9	4.1	3.7	4.2	3.7	5.5	4.8	–0.8	4.8	4.3
IMF	2.5	1.7	2.3	3.1	3.0	3.3	2.7	–0.6	4.3	1.2
Zone	54.2	50.1	52.5	54.6	59.5	77.1	78.1	1.0	74.7	60.6
Comoros	27.8	28.2	33.0	25.2	24.8	22.4	40.5	18.2	36.8	32.5
Of which: bilateral	10.5	12.0	14.4	7.5	8.3	4.9	17.1	12.2	11.1	9.6
multilateral	17.3	16.2	18.6	17.8	16.5	17.5	23.4	5.9	25.7	22.9
IMF	—	—	—	—	—	—	—	—	—	—

Sources: Data provided by the authorities; and Fund staff estimates and projections as of the end of May 1995.

Table 31. Total Government Revenue, 1990–96
(In percent of GDP)

	1990–93 Average	1990	1991	1992	1993	1994 Original program	1994 Provi-sional	1994 Deviation	1995 Program/ Projections	1996 Projections
WAEMU	17.3	18.6	17.8	17.1	15.4	16.6	15.9	–0.7	16.3	16.5
Benin	11.6	9.9	11.5	12.2	12.9	13.2	12.5	–0.7	12.6	12.9
Burkina Faso	12.5	12.3	13.3	11.8	12.6	11.5	11.0	–0.5	10.7	11.2
Côte d'Ivoire	21.8	23.4	21.9	22.3	19.6	22.4	22.5	—	22.2	21.7
Mali	15.3	17.2	16.3	13.7	13.9	13.2	13.4	0.2	13.5	14.4
Niger	8.6	10.3	8.5	8.2	7.3	8.9	6.2	–2.7	7.7	9.7
Senegal	18.4	19.4	19.8	18.2	16.1	16.1	14.0	–2.1	15.3	15.4
Togo	16.6	22.5	17.3	16.2	10.1	11.8	11.9	0.2	14.8	14.9
CAEMC	17.4	17.4	18.3	17.9	15.8	18.9	15.1	–3.7	17.8	18.6
Cameroon	14.9	14.9	15.8	16.3	12.7	15.8	9.5	–6.4	13.3	14.2
Central African Republic	9.4	10.9	9.6	9.2	8.0	9.8	7.3	–2.5	9.1	10.0
Chad	9.5	9.9	9.3	9.0	9.7	9.5	6.3	–3.2	9.0	9.8
Congo	23.3	27.0	25.3	22.5	18.4	27.5	24.7	–2.9	23.4	25.3
Equatorial Guinea	20.9	21.1	20.9	21.0	20.8	23.0	19.5	–3.6	18.5	19.3
Gabon	23.1	21.5	24.3	23.1	23.3	24.2	25.3	1.0	29.0	29.2
Zone	17.3	18.1	18.0	17.5	15.6	17.6	15.5	–2.1	17.0	17.4
Comoros	15.7	17.6	14.2	15.5	15.4	18.0	12.6	–5.4	15.4	15.7

Sources: Data provided by the authorities; and Fund staff estimates and projections as of the end of May 1995.
Note: Excluding grants.

Table 32. Total Government Tax Revenue, 1990–96
(In percent of GDP)

	1990–93 Average	1990	1991	1992	1993	1994 Original program	1994 Provi-sional	1994 Deviation	1995 Program/ Projections	1996 Projections
WAEMU	14.1	14.8	14.9	14.1	12.8	14.1	13.2	–0.9	13.6	14.0
Benin	9.8	8.7	9.4	10.3	10.9	11.7	10.8	–0.9	10.5	10.3
Burkina Faso	9.5	10.2	10.1	8.7	9.1	10.5	10.1	–0.4	10.0	9.5
Côte d'Ivoire	18.2	19.2	18.6	18.6	16.4	18.3	18.1	–0.2	17.7	17.9
Mali	10.9	9.8	12.3	10.6	11.1	11.0	9.9	–1.1	10.8	11.8
Niger	7.1	7.9	7.0	6.7	6.6	8.2	5.6	–2.6	7.0	8.9
Senegal	15.4	15.6	17.0	15.3	13.9	14.1	12.4	–1.6	13.3	14.1
Togo	13.5	18.5	15.1	12.3	8.1	10.8	11.1	0.3	12.7	13.2
CAEMC	16.3	16.7	17.3	16.6	14.7	17.6	14.2	–3.3	17.0	17.4
Cameroon	13.7	14.2	14.6	14.6	11.6	14.4	8.6	–5.8	12.3	13.0
Central African Republic	8.5	10.4	8.6	8.2	6.8	9.1	6.3	–2.8	8.2	9.0
Chad	7.9	9.5	7.4	7.3	7.5	8.2	5.7	–2.5	7.5	8.3
Congo	22.8	26.4	24.8	22.1	18.0	26.6	24.2	–2.5	22.6	24.6
Equatorial Guinea	13.9	14.2	13.6	14.0	14.0	13.1	13.0	–0.2	12.1	12.6
Gabon	22.2	20.6	23.7	22.3	22.3	23.3	24.3	1.0	28.7	28.1
Zone	15.1	15.7	16.0	15.2	13.6	15.6	13.7	–1.9	15.0	15.5
Comoros	12.5	12.3	11.1	13.3	13.4	16.0	11.1	–4.8	13.6	13.9

Sources: Data provided by the authorities; and Fund staff estimates and projections as of the end of May 1995.

Table 33. Domestic Tax Revenue, 1990–96
(In percent of GDP)

	1990–93 Average	1990	1991	1992	1993	1994 Original program	1994 Provisional	1994 Deviation	1995 Program/ Projections	1996 Projections
WAEMU	9.9	10.4	10.1	10.0	9.1	8.0	8.2	0.2	8.2	8.7
Benin	8.1	7.2	7.7	8.6	9.1	9.9	9.1	–0.8	8.8	8.6
Burkina Faso	6.1	6.6	6.3	5.7	6.0	6.0	5.9	–0.1	5.9	6.1
Côte d'Ivoire	14.4	14.9	14.1	15.2	13.3	10.8	11.5	0.6	11.0	11.6
Mali	6.7	7.0	7.2	6.2	6.3	5.7	5.9	0.2	6.1	6.8
Niger	3.7	3.9	3.7	3.8	3.5	4.1	2.9	–1.2	3.3	4.5
Senegal[1]	8.7	8.8	9.6	8.4	7.9	6.6	6.7	—	6.8	7.4
Togo	9.5	13.2	10.6	8.5	5.7	6.3	7.3	1.0	8.4	8.9
CAEMC	13.1	13.7	14.0	13.2	11.4	13.2	11.6	–1.5	13.4	13.6
Cameroon	11.4	12.1	12.2	11.9	9.3	10.8	6.9	–3.9	9.8	10.2
Central African Republic	5.0	6.0	4.9	5.0	4.1	4.6	3.9	–0.7	5.0	5.8
Chad	6.3	7.1	6.0	5.9	6.2	6.3	4.4	–1.9	5.4	5.9
Congo	18.2	22.0	20.4	17.3	13.0	19.1	20.9	1.8	17.4	19.9
Equatorial Guinea[2]	7.8	7.5	7.3	8.3	8.1	5.0	5.5	0.5	4.9	4.9
Gabon	17.7	16.7	18.6	17.9	17.6	18.4	20.2	1.8	23.5	22.1
Zone	11.3	11.9	11.9	11.4	10.1	10.2	9.7	–0.5	10.5	10.9
Comoros	4.2	5.0	4.5	4.1	3.1	3.9	3.0	–0.9	4.5	4.5

Sources: Data provided by the authorities; and Fund staff estimates and projections as of the end of May 1995.
Note: Including VAT turnover tax on imports unless otherwise indicated.
[1]Excluding VAT on imports for which no data are available.
[2]Including petroleum taxes.

Table 34. Tax on International Trade, 1990–96

(In percent of GDP)

	Tax on Exports										Tax on Imports[1]									
						1994			1995	1996						1994			1995	1996
	1990–93 Average	1990	1991	1992	1993	Original program	Provi-sional	Deviation	Program/ Projections	Projec-tions	1990–93 Average	1990	1991	1992	1993	Original program	Provi-sional	Deviation	Program/ Projections	Projec-tions
WAEMU	0.2	0.2	0.2	0.1	0.2	2.0	1.5	–0.5	1.6	1.4	4.1	4.2	4.6	3.9	3.6	4.1	3.6	–0.5	3.7	4.0
Benin	0.1	0.1	0.1	0.1	0.1	0.1	—	–0.1	—	—	1.6	1.4	1.5	1.6	1.8	1.7	1.6	–0.1	1.7	1.7
Burkina Faso	0.1	0.1	0.1	0.1	0.1	—	—	—	—	—	3.2	3.3	3.6	2.9	3.0	4.6	4.1	–0.5	4.1	4.5
Côte d'Ivoire	0.3	0.3	0.3	0.2	0.2	5.1	3.7	–1.3	4.2	3.6	3.6	3.9	4.2	3.3	2.9	2.4	2.9	0.5	2.4	2.7
Mali	—	—	—	—	—	—	—	—	—	—	4.2	2.8	4.9	4.4	4.8	5.3	4.0	–1.3	4.7	5.1
Niger	0.7	0.9	0.6	0.5	0.7	1.1	0.7	–0.4	1.0	1.2	2.4	3.0	2.4	2.1	2.2	3.0	2.0	–1.0	2.8	3.3
Senegal	—	—	—	—	—	—	—	—	—	—	6.8	6.7	7.5	6.9	6.0	7.4	5.8	–1.6	6.5	6.7
Togo	—	—	—	—	—	0.8	0.7	–0.1	0.7	0.4	4.0	5.3	4.5	3.7	2.4	3.4	3.1	–0.3	3.6	3.9
CAEMC	0.2	0.2	0.2	0.1	0.2	0.5	0.5	—	0.7	0.7	3.1	2.8	3.2	3.3	3.0	3.9	2.1	–1.8	2.7	2.9
Cameroon	0.1	0.1	0.1	0.1	0.1	0.5	0.5	—	0.7	0.8	2.3	2.0	2.3	2.7	2.1	3.1	1.2	–1.9	1.9	2.0
Central African Republic	0.5	0.6	0.6	0.5	0.4	1.3	0.6	–0.7	0.8	0.7	3.0	3.8	3.1	2.7	2.3	3.2	1.8	–1.4	2.5	2.5
Chad	0.1	0.1	0.1	0.1	0.2	—	0.2	0.2	—	—	1.5	2.3	1.3	1.3	1.2	1.9	1.1	–0.8	2.0	2.3
Congo	—	—	—	—	—	—	—	—	—	—	4.6	4.4	4.4	4.8	5.0	7.5	3.3	–4.2	5.2	5.0
Equatorial Guinea	2.0	2.5	1.9	1.7	2.0	3.1	3.8	0.7	3.7	3.6	4.2	4.4	4.1	4.0	4.1	4.9	3.6	–1.3	3.3	4.1
Gabon	0.3	0.2	0.3	0.1	0.4	0.7	0.6	–0.1	1.0	0.9	4.3	3.7	4.8	4.4	4.2	4.2	3.5	–0.7	3.5	4.3
Zone	0.2	0.2	0.2	0.1	0.2	1.4	1.0	–0.4	1.2	1.1	3.6	3.5	3.9	3.6	3.3	4.0	2.9	–1.1	3.3	3.5
Comoros	1.1	1.4	0.7	1.2	1.1	1.9	0.9	–1.0	0.9	0.9	7.4	6.0	5.9	8.7	9.2	10.1	7.3	–2.8	8.3	8.5

Sources: Data provided by the authorities; and Fund staff estimates and projections as of the end of May 1995.

[1]Excluding VAT turnover tax on imports, Senegal excepted.

Table 35. Total Government Expenditure, 1990–96
(In percent of GDP)

	1990–93 Average	1990	1991	1992	1993	1994 Original program	1994 Provi-sional	1994 Deviation	1995 Program/ Projections	1996 Projections
WAEMU	26.4	27.2	26.9	26.3	25.3	27.4	24.8	–2.6	23.4	22.3
Benin	19.1	19.9	18.7	20.2	17.6	24.1	19.3	–4.8	20.2	19.3
Burkina Faso	21.2	19.6	21.5	20.9	22.9	27.8	22.0	–5.8	20.5	19.9
Côte d'Ivoire	35.3	36.5	35.8	35.2	33.5	33.3	31.1	–2.2	28.7	26.7
Mali	25.7	25.8	28.6	24.9	23.5	28.2	26.8	–1.4	25.9	24.7
Niger	18.3	22.7	16.9	16.8	16.8	23.3	17.1	–6.2	17.9	18.1
Senegal	20.5	19.1	20.9	22.0	20.2	19.8	19.7	–0.1	17.9	17.7
Togo	25.2	28.7	25.3	22.1	24.6	26.4	24.2	–2.2	22.5	20.8
CAEMC	26.4	25.8	26.4	27.3	26.2	28.5	22.7	–5.8	22.0	21.1
Cameroon	22.5	22.9	22.8	23.2	21.1	22.9	17.1	–5.8	15.9	14.8
Central African Republic	24.1	22.7	26.9	24.7	22.0	23.5	22.4	–1.1	21.3	20.6
Chad	27.9	33.1	23.2	27.4	27.9	28.5	25.8	–2.7	24.3	24.4
Congo	38.5	34.3	39.6	41.4	38.6	46.1	37.5	–8.6	33.4	33.4
Equatorial Guinea	54.5	55.3	54.1	54.5	54.2	48.3	35.6	–12.7	40.5	32.3
Gabon	27.9	26.4	27.1	28.4	29.5	30.9	26.1	–4.8	29.0	27.7
Zone	26.4	26.5	26.7	26.8	25.7	27.8	23.9	–3.9	22.8	21.8
Comoros	32.5	34.2	33.4	35.0	27.6	34.6	33.9	–0.7	28.1	26.4

Sources: Data provided by the authorities; and Fund staff estimates and projections as of the end of May 1995.

Table 36. Basic Primary Expenditure, 1990–96
(In percent of GDP)

	1990–93 Average	1990	1991	1992	1993	1994 Original program	1994 Provi-sional	1994 Deviation	1995 Program/ Projections	1996 Projections
WAEMU	17.6	18.3	17.5	17.5	17.1	15.6	15.3	–0.3	14.2	13.4
Benin	11.0	11.2	11.0	11.0	10.8	12.6	10.2	–2.4	10.8	10.4
Burkina Faso	13.6	14.0	13.9	12.0	14.5	14.3	14.5	0.2	11.4	11.1
Côte d'Ivoire	22.9	24.6	22.4	22.7	22.0	19.0	19.3	0.3	18.0	16.9
Mali	15.9	17.2	17.2	14.9	14.1	13.8	13.4	–0.4	12.7	12.0
Niger	11.0	12.3	9.9	10.6	11.0	12.4	10.7	–1.7	10.9	10.1
Senegal	16.1	14.5	16.4	17.7	15.6	13.0	13.0	—	11.7	11.5
Togo	18.6	18.8	18.1	17.3	20.1	18.6	17.0	–1.6	15.6	14.0
CAEMC	17.8	16.7	17.5	19.0	18.1	14.6	12.5	–2.1	11.5	10.7
Cameroon	15.4	15.9	15.2	16.2	14.3	9.9	8.1	–1.8	7.2	6.8
Central African Republic	13.2	13.0	13.8	13.8	12.1	9.8	10.8	1.0	8.6	8.6
Chad	16.2	14.5	14.9	18.7	16.9	13.9	11.0	–2.9	10.7	10.9
Congo	27.3	20.1	28.8	31.1	29.1	25.7	22.2	–3.5	19.4	15.8
Equatorial Guinea	17.8	17.2	15.8	16.7	21.4	13.1	10.1	–3.0	11.5	12.2
Gabon	19.3	17.9	18.0	20.1	21.2	19.0	17.3	–1.7	17.9	17.0
Zone	17.7	17.5	17.5	18.2	17.5	15.2	14.0	–1.2	13.0	12.2
Comoros	18.6	19.6	20.2	19.0	15.6	16.5	17.0	0.5	14.3	14.4

Sources: Data provided by the authorities; and Fund staff estimates and projections as of the end of May 1995.

Note: Excluding interest payments due on domestic and foreign debt, foreign-financed investment, and net lending, but including domestically financed investment.

Table 37. Government Wage Bill, 1990–96
(In percent of GDP)

	1990–93 Average	1990	1991	1992	1993	1994 Original program	1994 Provi-sional	1994 Deviation	1995 Program/ Projections	1996 Projections
WAEMU	9.0	9.2	9.1	8.9	8.9	7.0	7.1	0.1	6.4	6.1
Benin	6.8	7.2	7.0	6.9	6.3	5.6	5.4	–0.2	4.9	5.0
Burkina Faso	6.9	7.6	6.9	6.4	6.6	5.5	5.6	0.1	5.2	4.8
Côte d'Ivoire	12.1	12.6	11.8	11.9	11.9	8.9	8.7	–0.2	7.8	7.3
Mali	5.8	5.7	6.3	5.6	5.4	4.3	4.3	—	4.1	3.8
Niger	6.0	5.4	5.9	6.3	6.4	5.2	5.5	0.3	5.3	5.0
Senegal	8.5	8.3	8.7	8.6	8.3	6.6	6.9	0.3	6.5	6.1
Togo	9.1	8.2	9.2	8.6	10.2	9.5	9.0	–0.5	7.7	7.4
CAEMC	9.6	8.7	9.8	10.3	9.8	7.3	6.5	–0.8	5.8	5.4
Cameroon	9.1	8.9	9.4	9.7	8.4	5.8	4.4	–1.4	3.8	3.5
Central African Republic	6.5	6.0	6.7	6.7	6.5	4.6	5.3	0.7	4.3	4.0
Chad	6.4	6.4	5.8	5.8	7.6	5.5	5.6	0.1	5.2	5.0
Congo	15.7	10.4	16.9	17.4	17.9	14.5	14.2	–0.3	11.8	10.0
Equatorial Guinea	6.0	6.1	6.3	6.0	5.9	4.3	4.0	–0.3	3.7	3.5
Gabon	9.2	8.5	8.7	9.9	9.9	7.9	7.8	–0.1	7.8	7.6
Zone	9.3	9.0	9.4	9.5	9.3	7.1	6.8	–0.3	6.1	5.8
Comoros	9.7	10.2	10.5	9.4	8.6	8.4	7.8	–0.6	7.6	7.4

Sources: Data provided by the authorities; and Fund staff estimates and projections as of the end of May 1995.

Table 38. Government Wage Bill, 1991–96
(Annual percentage changes)

	1991–93 Average	1991	1992	1993	1994 Original program	1994 Provi-sional	1994 Deviation	1995 Program/ Projections	1996 Projections
WAEMU	–0.9	–1.1	0.1	–1.7	10.1	9.9	–0.2	4.7	2.8
Benin	1.3	2.8	5.1	–3.8	16.2	21.2	5.0	10.5	9.3
Burkina Faso	–2.9	–5.4	–5.9	2.6	11.3	11.5	0.2	6.0	2.1
Côte d'Ivoire	–2.5	–6.5	0.7	–1.7	6.1	4.3	–1.8	2.8	1.5
Mali	2.5	11.0	–2.1	–1.4	10.0	8.8	–1.2	7.9	2.1
Niger	3.2	5.4	0.5	3.6	9.9	16.6	6.7	6.6	1.6
Senegal	0.8	4.2	2.7	–4.5	12.6	12.5	–0.1	5.8	1.6
Togo	2.2	15.1	–8.1	–0.3	25.7	27.8	2.1	3.0	11.0
CAEMC	2.3	11.3	3.1	–7.6	–7.5	–8.8	–1.3	–1.1	1.6
Cameroon	–5.6	1.1	0.5	–18.3	–19.1	–27.0	–7.9	0.7	0.6
Central African Republic	–1.0	5.9	–3.2	–5.7	—	11.7	11.7	–3.5	2.8
Chad	3.6	–2.0	1.0	11.8	10.1	10.1	—	6.0	4.5
Congo	22.8	63.7	3.8	0.8	–10.4	–3.7	6.7	–16.0	—
Equatorial Guinea	5.7	4.5	8.7	4.0	11.5	–3.8	–15.3	8.0	3.7
Gabon	6.1	5.2	9.5	3.7	10.0	10.0	—	7.9	3.0
Zone	0.5	4.5	1.5	–4.5	1.9	1.1	–0.8	2.3	2.3
Comoros	–3.3	5.9	–9.7	–6.2	9.8	13.1	3.3	2.9	4.2

Sources: Data provided by the authorities; and Fund staff estimates and projections as of the end of May 1995.

Table 39. Adjustments in Civil Service Wage Bill, 1993–95

	1993			1994			1995		
	Nominal salary	Allowances or other remuneration[1]	Net change in civil service employment	Nominal salary	Allowances or other remuneration[1]	Net change in civil service employment	Nominal salary	Allowances or other remuneration[1]	Net change in civil service employment
WAEMU									
Benin	Unchanged.	Unchanged.	–2,338 excluding military.	+10%	Restoration of the 10% housing allowance suspended in 1989; raises related to past promotions.	–688 excluding military.	Unchanged.	Increase in family allowance; expansion of housing allowance.	–223 until end of May, excluding military.
Burkina Faso	Unchanged.	Unchanged.	1,362 (+4%) excluding military.	+4–11% varying according to grade, effective 4/94.	+1.7%, mainly effect of wage drift.	3,327 (+9.3%) excluding military.	Unchanged.	Unchanged, through freezing of promotions.	800 (+2.1%), including +900 in education and health, excluding military.
Côte d'Ivoire	Unchanged.	Unchanged.	–2,700, including +700 in education and health, excluding military.	+10% effective 2/94 from 5% (highest wages) to 15% (lowest wages).	Unchanged.	–3,600, including +600 in education and health, excluding military.	+5.5% effective 5/95 from 1% (highest wages) to 13% (lowest wages).	Unchanged.	–2,900, including +2,400 in education and health, excluding military.
Mali	Unchanged.	Unchanged.	1,977 (–5.2%) excluding military.	+10% effective 4/94 and +5% effective 10/94.	Unchanged.	3,336 (–9%) excluding military.	Unchanged.	Unchanged.	. . .
Niger	–13.1% effective 8/93.	Unchanged.	120 (–0.3%) excluding military.	+15% effective 1/94 and +8% effective 4/94.	Unchanged.	1,202 (+3%) excluding military.	Unchanged.	Unchanged.	Some reduction programmed but magnitude not specified yet.
Senegal	–15% effective 9/93.	–15% effective 9/93.	1,766 (+2.7%) excluding military.	+15% effective 01/94, +10% effective 4/94.	+15% effective 01/94.	360 (–0.5%) excluding military.	Unchanged.	Unchanged.	. . .
Togo	Unchanged. But payment reduced because of civil service strikes.	Unchanged.	–91 excluding military.	Unchanged.	Retroactive promotion that had been deferred in 1993 because of strikes.	+296	Unchanged.	+4% resulting from the elimination of the national solidarity tax.	Study of possible overstaffing; recommendations expected by end. 1995.
CAEMC									
Cameroon	–15% effective 1/93 and –30% effective 11/93.	Unchanged.	–5,800 including military.	Unchanged.	Unchanged.	–3,400 including military.	Unchanged.	Unchanged.	–6,000 projected.
Central African Republic	–14% effective 5/93.	Unchanged.	. . .	+18% effective 3/94.	Unchanged.	–299 including military.	Unchanged.	Unchanged.	–657

Chad	Unchanged.	Unchanged.	. . .	+10% effective 6/94, offsetting the reduction by 10% in 1992.	Family allowances not paid.	–500 (including increase in education (280) and health (90) but excluding military).	General increase by 10%, effective 95.	Family allowances not paid.	Unchanged. Hirings in education and health sectors offset by retirements.
Congo	Unchanged.	Unchanged.	–1,200 including military.	Unchanged.	Unchanged.	–6,900	–12.5% excluding military, teachers, & diplomats, 15% except wages below CFAF 50,000.	–30% on about 50% of benefits.	–1,000
Equatorial Guinea	Unchanged.	Unchanged.	. . .	+14% effective 6/94.	Unchanged.	–380 excluding military.	Unchanged.	Severance pay equal to 80% salary indefinitely.	Unchanged, excluding military.
Gabon	Unchanged.	Unchanged.	–329 including military (42).	+8.5% effective 4/94.	Unchanged.	+1,520 including military (78).	Unchanged.	Unchanged.	+380 including military (300) as of 5/95.

[1]All nonbase salary remuneration.

Table 40. Government Investment Expenditure, 1990–96
(In percent of GDP)

	1990–93 Average	1990	1991	1992	1993	1994 Original program	1994 Provi-sional	1994 Deviation	1995 Program/ Projections	1996 Projections
WAEMU	4.9	4.7	5.0	5.1	4.7	7.1	5.9	–1.2	6.4	6.7
Benin	4.9	5.4	5.3	4.2	4.7	9.2	6.4	–2.8	7.6	7.4
Burkina Faso	7.4	5.6	7.1	8.9	8.0	12.3	7.0	–5.3	8.3	8.6
Côte d'Ivoire	3.2	2.8	3.2	3.3	3.4	5.2	5.2	—	5.4	5.8
Mali	9.3	9.2	10.3	8.9	9.0	13.2	12.3	–0.9	12.6	12.5
Niger	5.8	8.9	5.4	4.7	4.3	8.2	4.2	–4.0	4.9	5.6
Senegal	4.2	2.9	4.6	5.1	4.1	4.9	4.6	–0.3	4.8	5.1
Togo	4.3	7.2	4.5	3.5	2.2	3.0	2.2	–0.8	3.8	4.7
CAEMC	5.1	6.1	4.8	4.5	4.9	6.5	3.9	–2.6	4.6	4.9
Cameroon	4.3	5.6	4.2	3.7	3.9	3.3	1.7	–1.6	2.0	2.3
Central African Republic	9.6	9.4	10.2	9.9	9.0	11.5	10.1	–1.4	11.3	11.0
Chad	10.8	18.2	7.5	7.9	9.9	13.8	13.3	–0.5	12.3	12.1
Congo	1.5	2.7	0.9	0.8	1.7	8.0	3.1	–4.9	2.7	4.8
Equatorial Guinea	31.8	35.0	33.2	32.1	26.9	28.7	19.0	–9.7	26.0	18.7
Gabon	5.3	4.6	5.5	5.5	5.7	7.6	4.6	–3.0	6.6	6.7
Zone	5.0	5.3	4.9	4.8	4.8	6.9	5.0	–1.9	5.6	5.9
Comoros	8.2	6.3	6.9	12.2	7.5	9.4	9.3	–0.1	6.3	5.7

Sources: Data provided by the authorities; and Fund staff estimates and projections as of the end of May 1995.
Note: Excluding net lending.

Table 41. Public Investment Financed by Internal Resources, 1990–96
(In percent of GDP)

	1990–93 Average	1990	1991	1992	1993	1994 Original program	1994 Provi-sional	1994 Deviation	1995 Program/ Projections	1996 Projections
WAEMU	1.4	1.1	1.4	1.8	1.4	1.6	1.6	—	1.6	1.7
Benin	0.3	0.2	0.3	0.3	0.5	1.2	0.5	–0.7	0.9	1.3
Burkina Faso	1.1	1.1	0.8	1.5	1.1	1.0	0.9	–0.1	0.9	1.4
Côte d'Ivoire	1.8	1.6	1.8	2.3	1.7	2.3	2.7	0.4	2.6	2.5
Mali	0.8	0.7	0.7	0.7	1.2	1.3	1.2	–0.1	1.3	1.4
Niger	0.4	0.9	0.3	0.2	0.2	0.4	0.2	–0.2	0.2	0.3
Senegal	2.0	0.8	2.4	2.9	1.8	1.7	1.2	–0.5	1.4	1.8
Togo	1.1	0.7	0.5	1.5	1.6	0.4	0.6	0.2	0.7	0.5
CAEMC	2.0	1.7	1.5	2.1	2.7	1.5	1.3	–0.2	1.3	1.3
Cameroon	2.0	1.8	1.4	2.0	2.7	0.5	0.3	–0.2	0.4	0.5
Central African Republic	1.8	2.1	2.2	1.5	1.5	1.6	1.2	–0.4	1.2	1.5
Chad	0.3	0.2	0.2	0.3	0.4	0.9	0.2	–0.7	0.3	0.7
Congo	0.7	0.2	0.1	0.8	1.7	0.8	2.2	1.4	—	—
Equatorial Guinea	2.2	3.3	1.9	1.9	1.6	1.8	1.1	–0.7	1.8	1.7
Gabon	3.0	2.3	2.4	3.6	3.8	3.3	3.2	–0.1	3.9	3.6
Zone	1.7	1.3	1.4	1.9	1.9	1.5	1.5	—	1.5	1.6
Comoros	1.4	1.2	0.9	1.9	1.5	0.8	0.7	–0.1	0.7	0.7

Sources: Data provided by the authorities; and Fund staff estimates and projections as of the end of May 1995.

Table 42. Basic Primary Balance, 1990–96

(In percent of GDP)

	1990–93 Average	1990	1991	1992	1993	1994 Original program	1994 Provi-sional	1994 Deviation	1995 Program/ Projections	1996 Projections
WAEMU	–0.3	0.4	0.3	–0.4	–1.6	1.0	0.6	–0.4	2.1	3.1
Benin	0.7	–1.3	0.5	1.3	2.2	0.7	2.3	1.6	1.9	2.5
Burkina Faso	–1.1	–1.6	–0.5	–0.3	–1.9	–2.8	–3.5	–0.7	–0.7	0.1
Côte d'Ivoire	–1.1	–1.2	–0.5	–0.4	–2.4	3.5	3.2	–0.3	4.1	4.9
Mali	–0.6	—	–0.9	–1.3	–0.3	–0.6	–0.1	0.5	0.8	2.4
Niger	–2.4	–2.1	–1.4	–2.4	–3.7	–3.4	–4.5	–1.1	–3.2	–0.4
Senegal	2.3	4.9	3.5	0.5	0.5	3.1	1.0	–2.1	3.6	3.8
Togo	–2.0	3.7	–0.8	–1.0	–10.0	–6.7	–5.1	1.6	–0.9	0.9
CAEMC	–0.5	0.8	0.7	–1.1	–2.2	4.7	2.7	–2.0	6.3	7.7
Cameroon	–0.5	–1.0	0.6	0.1	–1.6	5.9	1.4	–4.5	6.1	7.4
Central African Republic	–4.5	–2.1	–6.9	–4.8	–4.1	—	–3.5	–3.5	0.5	1.3
Chad	–6.8	–4.6	–5.6	–9.8	–7.1	–4.4	–4.7	–0.3	–1.8	–1.1
Congo	–4.0	6.9	–3.5	–8.6	–10.7	1.8	2.5	0.7	3.9	9.5
Equatorial Guinea	3.6	4.2	5.2	4.3	0.7	10.0	9.3	–0.7	7.1	7.1
Gabon	3.8	3.6	6.3	3.0	2.1	6.9	8.0	1.1	11.1	11.4
Zone	–0.4	0.6	0.5	–0.7	–1.9	2.6	1.5	–1.1	4.0	5.1
Comoros	–2.9	–2.0	–6.0	–3.5	–0.3	1.5	–4.4	–5.9	1.1	1.3

Sources: Data provided by the authorities; and Fund staff estimates and projections as of the end of May 1995.

Note: Excluding grants, interest payments on domestic and foreign debt, foreign-financed investment, and net lending, but including domestically financed investment.

Table 43. Overall Fiscal Balance, 1990–96

(In percent of GDP)

	1990–93 Average	1990	1991	1992	1993	1994 Original program	1994 Provi-sional	1994 Deviation	1995 Program/ Projections	1996 Projections
WAEMU	–6.8	–6.2	–6.8	–6.8	–7.5	–7.5	–5.7	1.8	–4.3	–4.6
Benin	–3.2	–4.1	–3.9	–3.8	–0.8	–3.3	–2.2	1.1	–2.5	–2.0
Burkina Faso	–4.0	–4.6	–3.6	–2.9	–4.9	–6.4	–3.7	2.7	–3.9	–5.0
Côte d'Ivoire	–13.3	–13.1	–13.9	–12.9	–13.3	–10.1	–7.8	2.3	–5.5	–4.0
Mali	–3.7	–2.7	–3.9	–3.9	–4.1	–9.2	–8.1	1.1	–7.1	–5.2
Niger	–4.8	–7.0	–3.6	–4.7	–3.8	–9.0	–6.7	2.3	–6.2	–5.2
Senegal	–0.8	2.0	0.2	–2.5	–3.0	–2.4	–1.8	0.6	–1.1	–1.2
Togo	–6.9	–2.9	–6.5	–4.1	–14.2	–13.5	–9.4	4.1	–4.6	–4.0
CAEMC	–7.9	–7.0	–6.7	–8.5	–9.3	–7.0	–6.4	0.6	–2.8	–1.1
Cameroon	–7.4	–8.0	–6.3	–6.9	–8.4	–4.7	–7.4	–2.7	–2.3	–0.1
Central African Republic	–8.4	–7.0	–11.5	–8.4	–6.6	–4.8	–8.0	–3.2	–6.2	–5.3
Chad	–9.4	–8.2	–6.8	–11.7	–11.1	–11.1	–11.6	–0.5	–8.1	–7.8
Congo	–15.1	–7.0	–14.1	–19.0	–20.1	–17.3	–12.6	4.7	–8.9	–7.1
Equatorial Guinea	–10.8	–6.1	–5.4	–16.9	–14.7	–5.6	–2.5	3.1	–2.9	2.7
Gabon	–4.5	–4.5	–2.5	–5.2	–5.9	–6.2	–0.4	5.8	0.4	1.9
Zone	–7.3	–6.6	–6.8	–7.6	–8.3	–7.3	–6.0	1.3	–3.7	–2.5
Comoros	–1.2	–1.1	–2.6	–4.2	3.0	–4.0	–6.7	–2.7	–3.3	–1.0

Sources: Data provided by the authorities; and Fund staff estimates and projections as of the end of May 1995.

Note: Including grants.

Table 44. Monetary Survey, 1993

(Annual changes in percent of beginning-of-period money stock, except velocity)

	Net Foreign Assets	Net Domestic Assets	Domestic Credit: Total	Domestic Credit: Net central government	Broad Money	Velocity[1]
WAEMU[2]	0.9	–3.5	–4.1	–1.1	–2.6	3.7
Benin	5.8	0.1	1.6	–1.6	5.9	4.0
Burkina Faso	9.8	–1.7	–2.1	3.5	8.1	4.3
Côte d'Ivoire	2.7	–7.1	0.7	28.8	–4.4	3.5
Mali	56.2	–47.8	98.9	28.5	8.4	4.4
Niger	–3.2	3.0	–24.3	–7.1	–0.1	5.1
Senegal	–8.0	–4.5	–3.2	–6.6	–12.6	4.7
Togo	–20.7	5.9	–9.1	5.1	–14.9	2.2
CAEMC[2]	–3.9	–5.9	–8.4	3.5	–9.8	5.8
Cameroon	–9.8	1.1	–3.9	6.0	–8.8	5.4
Central African Republic	13.4	–0.6	–13.1	2.6	12.9	6.1
Chad	–23.2	1.6	11.5	21.2	–21.6	6.3
Congo	0.5	–5.1	19.9	10.3	–4.6	4.1
Equatorial Guinea	–26.1	36.0	68.6	69.9	9.9	12.6
Gabon	–14.0	12.3	40.0	40.2	–1.8	4.4
Comoros	21.3	–17.9	–12.9	–10.4	3.4	4.2

Sources: Data provided by the authorities; and Fund staff estimates and projections as of the end of May 1995.

Note: Actual.

[1]GDP/end of year broad money.

[2]Definition BCEAO or BEAC.

Table 45. Monetary Survey, 1994

(Annual changes in percent of beginning-of-period money stock, except velocity)

	Net Foreign Assets			Net Domestic Assets			Domestic Credit: Total			Domestic Credit: Net central government			Broad money (M2)			Velocity[1]		
	Original program	Provisional	Deviation	Original program	Provisional	Deviation	Original program	Provisional	Deviation	Original program	Provisional	Deviation	Original program	Provisional	Deviation	Original program	Provisional	Deviation
WAEMU[2]	. . .	33.0	. . .	. . .	7.2	. . .	. . .	6.1	. . .	. . .	2.2	. . .	. . .	40.2	. . .	. . .	3.7	. . .
Benin	17.5	50.9	33.4	12.0	–8.3	–20.3	12.1	6.8	–5.3	–2.8	–5.7	–2.9	29.5	42.6	13.1	4.8	4.1	–0.7
Burkina Faso	11.2	26.7	15.5	9.6	2.9	–6.7	16.3	–2.1	–18.4	2.5	6.2	3.7	20.8	29.6	8.8	4.6	4.3	–0.3
Côte d'Ivoire	24.4	65.8	41.4	10.9	–18.4	–29.3	8.3	–5.5	–13.8	–11.3	–15.3	–4.0	35.1	47.4	12.3	3.9	3.5	–0.4
Mali	24.8	31.0	6.2	12.0	6.7	–5.3	12.0	7.7	–4.3	0.5	–0.4	–0.9	36.8	37.7	0.9	4.5	4.4	–0.1
Niger	21.3	17.1	–4.2	5.7	7.9	2.2	31.2	31.2	—	18.2	20.8	2.6	27.0	25.0	–2.0	5.6	5.7	0.1
Senegal	12.9	46.1	33.2	21.3	–6.6	–27.9	24.4	–5.1	–29.5	–3.1	–13.3	–10.2	34.2	39.2	5.0	5.3	4.6	–0.7
Togo	8.0	22.2	14.2	23.0	6.1	–16.9	23.9	10.8	–13.1	10.1	11.3	1.2	31.0	28.4	–2.6	3.0	3.3	0.3
CAEMC[2]	. . .	24.4	. . .	. . .	8.3	. . .	. . .	11.6	. . .	. . .	10.8	. . .	. . .	32.8	. . .	. . .	6.0	. . .
Cameroon	–9.3	23.9	33.2	30.5	4.2	–26.3	30.5	1.5	–29.0	6.7	2.1	–4.6	21.2	28.1	6.9	6.1	6.7	0.6
Central African Republic	5.5	66.4	60.9	19.0	12.0	–7.0	25.5	11.6	–13.9	10.9	6.0	–4.9	24.5	78.5	54.0	6.4	4.9	–1.5
Chad	–2.8	31.3	34.1	29.0	0.2	–28.8	29.0	14.8	–14.2	14.2	8.1	–6.1	26.2	31.5	5.3	6.1	7.1	1.0
Congo	4.8	13.8	9.0	7.9	14.4	6.5	7.9	–1.2	–9.1	–4.8	–6.8	–2.0	12.5	28.2	15.7	4.6	4.2	–0.4
Equatorial Guinea	26.0	51.4	25.4	12.9	89.0	76.1	6.1	52.0	45.9	–22.3	36.3	58.6	38.9	140.3	101.4	13.0	8.1	–4.9
Gabon	10.1	50.8	40.7	9.7	–14.1	–23.8	9.1	–6.0	–15.1	–8.8	–4.8	4.0	19.8	36.7	16.9	4.6	3.7	–0.9
Comoros	41.4	26.7	–14.7	–22.4	–21.3	1.1	9.4	10.3	0.9	–1.8	5.4	7.2	19.0	5.4	–13.6	4.2	4.9	0.7

Sources: Data provided by the authorities; and Fund staff estimates and projections as of the end of May 1995.

[1]GDP/end-of-year broad money.

[2]Definition BCEAO or BEAC.

Table 46. Interest Rate Structure, 1989–95

(In percent per year, end of period)

		1989	1990	1991	1992	1993	1/14/94	6/94	12/94	3/95	6/95
Central Bank interest rates											
Money market rate[1]	WAEMU	10.975	10.975	10.85	12.1	7.35	9.25	8.0	5.5	5.5	5.5
	CAEMC	10.0	11.0	10.75	12.0	11.5	14.0	12.5	7.75	8.0	8.75
Repo rate[1]	WAEMU	—	—	—	—	8.75	12.75	10.25	7.0	7.0	6.5
	CAEMC[2]	—	—	—	—	—	—	—	9.25	10.0	10.5
Penalty rate[3]	WAEMU	11.0	11.0	11.0	12.5	10.5	14.5	12.0	10.0	9.0	8.5
	CAEMC	16.0	16.0	16.0	16.0	18.0	22.0	20.0	15.0	15.0	15.0
Rates on Treasury advances											
Normal rate	WAEMU	9.975	9.975	9.725	9.0	9.7	7.8	8.1	4.5	4.5	4.5
	CAEMC	4.5	5.5	7.5	9.5	11.0	11.0	11.0	7.75	7.75	8.0
Penalty rate[4]	WAEMU	. . .	. . .	12.5	12.5	9.25	13.25	13.25	7.5	7.5	7.5
	CAEMC	5.5	6.5	8.5	10.5	12.0	12.0	12.0	10.5	10.5	10.5
Deposits and lending rates											
Maximum lending rate	WAEMU[5]	16.0	16.0	16.0	17.5	21.0	29.0	24.0	20.0	18.0	17.0
	CAEMC[6]	—	—	18.25	17.5	17.5	19.0	17.0	16.0	16.0	16.0
Minimum rate on savings deposits	WAEMU	7.5	7.0	7.0	8.5	4.5	8.0	8.0	4.5	4.5	4.5
	CAEMC[6]	—	—	7.5	7.5	7.75	9.0	8.0	5.5	5.5	5.5
Deposits with the Central Bank[7]											
Commercial banks	CAEMC	9.75	10.75	9.75	9.75	9.75	9.75	9.75	4.0	4.2	4.5
Treasuries	CAEMC	. . .	5.0	7.0	9.0	10.5	10.5	10.5	4.0	4.2	4.5
Memorandum item:											
French money market overnight rate		11.0	10.0	10.75	10.75	6.69	6.43	5.44	5.38	7.75	7.12

Sources: BCEAO and BEAC.

[1]Before July 1994, there was no money market in the BEAC zone; the basic refinancing rate was the discount rate fixed administratively by the Governor. Following the introduction of the money market in July 1994, the discount rate was replaced by two rates, the auction rate and the rate for the repurchase agreements. Auctions of central bank money are organized weekly; the auction rate is, however, still set by the Governor.

[2]Set at 150 to 200 basis points above the auction rate.

[3]The penalty rate applies to nonreimbursed advances on the money market or as a sanction on an individual bank. Since October 1993, the penalty rate in the BCEAO zone is called the discount rate.

[4]Applies to advances to treasuries above the statutory ceiling.

[5]Since October 1993, the usury rate is twice the discount rate in the BCEAO.

[6]In the CAEMC, minimum and maximum rates varied across countries before 1991. The minimum deposit rate is applicable only to time deposits and savings bonds.

[7]Rate of remuneration of free reserves with the Central Bank. The BCEAO does not remunerate reserves.

Table 47. Sources of Exceptional Financial Assistance, 1993–94

(In millions of U.S. dollars)

	1993 Actuals	1994 Original program	1994 Provisional	1994 Deviation
Multilaterals and regional	247.1	2,504.6	2,163.3	−341.3
IMF	51.0	604.4	507.7	−96.7
World Bank	41.1	1,165.6	986.3	−179.3
African Development Bank	74.4	364.9	383.2	18.3
E. U. (incl. STABEX)	80.5	369.7	286.1	−83.6
Bilateral	921.0	934.0	579.0	−355.0
France	749.3	734.3	568.0	−166.3
Other countries	171.7	199.7	11.0	−188.7
Subtotal	1,168.1	3,438.6	2,742.3	−696.3
Debt relief	481.6	6,794.7	6,991.6	196.9
Project aid	1,756.8	1,798.9	1,369.1	−429.8
Total	3,406.5	12,032.2	11,103.0	−929.2

Sources: Data provided by the authorities; and Fund staff estimates as of the end of May 1995.

Table 48. Exceptional Financial Assistance by Recipient Country, 1993–94

(In millions of U.S. dollars)

	1993 Actuals	1994 Original program	1994 Provisional	1994 Deviation
WAEMU	840.2	2,043.2	1,738.6	−304.6
Benin	94.1	109.4	80.5	−28.9
Burkina Faso	91.2	178.1	149.1	−29.0
Côte d'Ivoire	507.0	1,100.0	1,050.7	−49.3
Mali	61.8	192.5	173.0	−19.5
Niger	79.8	166.9	99.1	−67.8
Senegal	6.3	204.7	131.5	−73.2
Togo	—	91.6	54.7	−36.9
CAEMC	327.9	1,395.4	1,003.7	−391.7
Cameroon	280.7	526.5	372.3	−154.2
Central African Republic	24.7	92.3	54.4	−37.9
Chad	12.9	99.0	63.5	−35.5
Congo	—	373.0	300.4	−72.6
Equatorial Guinea	9.6	11.2	2.6	−8.6
Gabon	—	293.4	210.5	−82.9
Zone	1,168.1	3,438.6	2,742.3	−696.3
Comoros	15.2	17.2	7.8	−9.4

Sources: Data provided by the authorities; and Fund staff estimates as of the end of May 1995.
Note: Including IMF.

Table 49. Project Aid by Recipient Country, 1993–94

(In millions of U.S. dollars)

	1993	1994		
	Actuals	Original program	Provisional	Deviation
WAEMU	1,215.7	1,257.7	1,054.4	–203.3
Benin	131.1	136.1	98.3	–37.8
Burkina Faso	201.8	222.8	112.6	–110.2
Côte d'Ivoire	155.3	180.2	167.5	–12.7
Mali	212.6	238.1	230.5	–7.6
Niger	89.7	110.6	61.6	–49.0
Senegal	417.4	345.6	367.3	21.7
Togo	7.8	24.3	16.6	–7.7
CAEMC	541.1	541.2	314.7	–226.5
Cameroon	120.9	105.8	60.7	–45.1
Central African Republic	70.6	70.4	77.5	7.1
Chad	217.9	98.7	103.3	4.6
Congo	—	101.7	16.2	–85.5
Equatorial Guinea	43.4	30.1	20.3	–9.8
Gabon	88.3	134.5	36.7	–97.8
Zone	1,756.8	1,798.9	1,369.1	–429.8
Comoros	20.6	21.5	18.9	–2.6

Sources: Data provided by the authorities; and Fund staff estimates as of the end of May 1995.
Note: As recorded in the balance of payments.

Table 50. Official Debt Relief by Recipient Country, 1993–94

(In millions of U.S. dollars)

	1993	1994		
	Actuals	Original program	Provisional	Deviation
WAEMU	192.1	1,958.0	2,203.2	245.2
Benin	27.8	35.5	42.7	7.2
Burkina Faso	12.0	26.3	13.8	–12.5
Côte d'Ivoire	—	1,212.9	1,512.5	299.6
Mali	108.1	78.6	93.3	14.7
Niger	9.2	151.7	194.7	43.0
Senegal	35.0	326.1	340.2	14.1
Togo	—	126.9	6.0	–120.9
CAEMC	289.5	4,836.7	4,788.4	–48.3
Cameroon	16.2	1,141.3	1,516.2	374.9
Central African Republic	—	76.2	81.3	5.1
Chad	—	40.3	7.4	–32.9
Congo[1]	273.3	2,032.5	1,688.0	–344.5
Equatorial Guinea	—	55.8	—	–55.8
Gabon	—	1,490.6	1,495.5	4.9
Zone	481.6	6,794.7	6,991.6	196.9
Comoros	14.0	19.7	8.2	–11.5

Sources: Data provided by the authorities; and Fund staff estimates as of the end of May 1995.
Note: Paris Club and implicitly other official bilateral creditors on similar terms. The 1994–95 agreement for Chad, Equatorial Guinea, and Togo are effective only from 1995 (see Table 28). Except for the rescheduling of Gabon's debt and part of the collateralized debt of the Congo, no formal agreement has been concluded yet with foreign commercial banks and other private creditors.
[1]Excluding the restructuring of commercial and other nonofficial collateralized debt.

Table 51. Disbursements from the Fund, 1994–95
(In millions of SDRs)

	Quota	Type of Arrangement		Date of Arrangement	Expiration Date	Amount Approved	Disbursements		Undrawn Balance
		1994	1995				1994	1995[1]	
WAEMU	618.1					775.3	246.1	123.1	353.6
Benin	45.3	ESAF II	ESAF III	January 25, 1993	January 24, 1996	51.9	18.1	9.1	9.1
Burkina Faso	44.2	ESAF II	ESAF III	March 31, 1993	March 30, 1996	48.6	9.8	8.8	13.3
Côte d'Ivoire	238.2	ESAF I	ESAF II	March 11, 1994	March 10, 1997	333.5	119.1	59.6	154.8
Mali	68.9	ESAF II	ESAF III	August 28, 1992	August 27, 1995	79.2	29.5	14.7	14.7
Niger	48.3	SBA	SBA	March 4, 1994	March 3, 1995	18.6	11.1	—	7.5
Senegal	118.9	SBA	—	March 2, 1994	August 29,1994	47.6	30.9	—	16.7
		ESAF I	ESAF II	August 29, 1994	August 28, 1997	130.8	16.7	30.9	83.2
Togo	54.3	ESAF I	ESAF II	September 16, 1994	September 16, 1997	65.2	10.9	10.9	54.3
CAEMC	410.1					188.7	80.3	22.1	105.5
Cameroon	135.1	SBA	SBA	March 14, 1994	September 13, 1995	81.1	21.9	—	59.2
Central African Republic	41.2	SBA	SBA	March 28, 1994	March 27, 1995	16.5	10.7	—	5.8
Chad	41.3	SBA	SBA	March 23, 1994	March 22, 1995	16.5	10.3	—	6.2
Congo	57.9	SBA	SBA	May 27, 1994	May 26, 1995	23.2	12.5	—	10.7
Equatorial Guinea	24.3	ESAF II		February 3, 1993	February 2, 1996	12.9	1.7	—	8.3
Gabon	110.3	SBA	SBA	March 30, 1994	March 29, 1995	38.6	23.2	22.1	15.4
Zone	1,028.2					964.0	326.4	145.2	459.1
Comoros	6.5	SAF		June 21, 1991	June 20, 1994	3.2	1.4	—	1.8

Source: IMF Treasurer's Department as of June 30, 1995.
[1]As of the end of June 1995.

Table 52. Official Producer Prices for Main Export Crops by Country, 1993–95
(Percentage changes)

	Cotton			Cocoa			Coffee			Others		
	1992/93	1993/94[1]	1994/95	1992/93	1993/94[1]	1994/95	1992/93	1993/94[1]	1994/95	1992/93	1993/94[1]	1994/95
WAEMU												
Benin	0	33	29	—	—	—	—	—	—	—	—	—
Burkina Faso	–11	40	25	—	—	—	—	—	—	—	—	—
Côte d'Ivoire	0	19	12	0	36	27	16	68	47	—	—	—
Mali	0	47	4	—	—	—	—	—	—	—	—	—
Niger[2]	—	—	—	—	—	—	—	—	—	–9	71	0
Senegal[3]	–15	29	36	—	—	—	—	—	—	–13	43	20
Togo	–10	22	32	–10	122	10	–24	61	189	—	—	—
CAEMC												
Cameroon	0	53	0	–25	100	0	35	100	0	—	—	—
Central African Republic	0	50	0				–20	200	100	—	—	—
Chad	0	13	33	—	—	—	—	—	—	—	—	—
Congo	—	—	—	—	—	—	—	—	—	—	—	—
Equatorial Guinea[4]	—	—	—	—	70	0	0	70	0	0	100	0
Gabon		—	—	—	30	0	0	30	0	—	—	—
Comoros[5]		—	—	—	—	—	—	—	—	–32	0	0

Sources: Data provided by the authorities; and Fund staff estimates and projections as of the end of May 1995.
[1]In 1994, the price increases took place after the January devaluation.
[2]For others: Uranium.
[3]For others: Groundnuts.
[4]For others: Timber.
[5]For others: Vanilla.

Table 53. Selected Demographic and Social Indicators

(Latest available data)

	Benin	Burkina Faso	Côte d'Ivoire	Mali	Niger	Senegal	Togo	Cameroon	C.A.R.	Chad	Congo	Equatorial Guinea	Gabon	Comoros
Population														
Total (million)	5.4	9.5	12.9	8.9	8.3	7.8	3.9	12.5	2.3	6.0	2.4	0.4	1.2	0.6
Growth rate	3.2	3.0	4.0	3.0	3.3	2.8	3.0	2.7	3.0	2.4	3.2	2.0	2.8	3.8
Percentage of urban population	39.6	17.0	42.0	25.0	21.0	40.8	29.0	43.1	48.0	34.0	42.0	29.0	47.0	29.5
Life expectancy (at birth)	51	47	56	48	46	49	55	56	47	48	51	48	54	56
Crude birthrate (per thousand)	45.0	—	—	50.1	—	45.4	—	—	—	—	—	—	—	—
Crude death rate (per thousand)	15.0	—	—	18.7	—	16.5	—	—	—	—	—	—	—	—
GNP per capita (US$ 1993)	430	300	630	270	270	750	340	820	400	210	950	420	4,960	430
Education							*(In percent)*							
Primary school enrollment rate (in percent)	62	37	81	32	29	59	111	101	68	65	—	—	—	75
Secondary school enrollment rate (in percent)	36	8	24	7	7	16	23	28	12	7	—	—	—	17
Primary pupil-to-teacher ratio														
Primary	35	60	37	47	38	58	59	51	—	64	66	—	44	45
Secondary	33	39	43	16	35	35	—	28	—	35	—	—	32	31
Health														
Population per physician (in thousands)	20.7	57.2	14.3	19.4	34.8	17.6	—	12.0	—	30.0	—	—	—	7.6
Population per hospital bed (in thousands)	—	3.4	1.3	1.4	—	1.4	0.7	0.4	—	1.3	—	—	—	—
Infant mortality rate (per thousand)	131	132	91	130	123	68	85	61	105	122	114	117	94	87
Access to safe water (in percent of population)														
Total	49	67	83	49	59	55	71	34	12	—	—	—	72	55
Urban	—	44	100	100	100	79	100	47	14	—	—	—	90	—
Rural	—	72	75	36	52	38	61	27	11	—	—	—	50	—
Nutrition														
Calorie intake per capita	—	—	—	2,314	2,308	2,369	—	—	—	—	—	—	—	—
Food production per capita index (average growth rate in percent, 1987=100)	118	112	89	91	128	81	100	89	93	111	96	—	98	90
Labor force														
Labor force (thousand)	2,311	4,442	4,840	3,130	3,817	3,329	1,469	4,663	1,436	2,096	820	189	546	250
Employment in agricultural sector (in percent of labor force)	—	—	65	86	85	81	—	—	—	—	—	—	—	—

Source: World Bank.

Annex II Economic Integration Within the Two Unions of the CFA Franc Zone

Economic and Monetary Unions[1]

Institutional Aspects

The devaluation of the CFA franc in January 1994 was the occasion for the member countries of the CFA franc zone to reaffirm their commitment to regional economic integration. The current initiatives aim at strengthening economic cooperation with a view to transforming the existing monetary arrangements into full-fledged economic and monetary unions. On January 10, 1994, the Heads of State of the West African Monetary Union (WAMU) signed the treaty establishing the West African Economic and Monetary Union (WAEMU); and on March 16, 1994, the Heads of State of the member countries of the Bank of Central African States (BEAC) signed a treaty setting up the Central African Economic and Monetary Community (CAEMC).[2] In addition, as part of an effort to improve the legal and regulatory framework in the CFA franc zone, initiatives have been taken to establish regional institutions capable of enforcing regional regulations in critical areas.

The treaty establishing the WAEMU became effective on August 1, 1994. Preparatory work had been conducted since 1992 by a Steering Committee that included officials of the seven countries and representatives of the donor community. The treaty sets up a new institutional framework, largely inspired by the European Union, with an executive committee consisting of seven members (the Commission) and jurisdictional organisms. The Commission was installed in Ouagadougou on January 30, 1995, and the legal, administrative, and financial framework under which WAEMU institutions will operate was adopted in August 1995.

In the Central African subregion, progress toward establishing a full-fledged economic and monetary union has been slower, although the first steps were initiated at end-1991. Following meetings of a group of national experts in 1991–92, the Governor of the BEAC presented a report to the Heads of State in December 1992 that led to the preparation of two draft conventions in the economic and monetary areas. In March 1994, the Heads of State of the six member countries signed the CAEMC treaty in N'Djaména joined by Cameroon in June 1994. The treaty itself, however, sets up only a legal framework, which is to be fleshed out by the two conventions on the Central African Monetary Union (CAMU) (and the attendant revision of the statutes of the BEAC) and the Central African Economic Union (CAEU).

In both subregions, the objectives of the treaties are the establishment of a common market based on a customs union and the harmonization of indirect tax legislation, and the coordination of economic policies between member countries through inter alia regional surveillance procedures. In addition, both treaties provide for the implementation in due course of common sectoral policies (in agriculture, human resources, manufacturing, transport, energy, and the environment). The pace of implementation of treaty dispositions has been uneven so far, with WAEMU countries taking a lead in multilateral surveillance matters, and CAEMC countries making more rapid progress toward a common customs union. Detailed measures included in the treaties and draft conventions, as well as a status of implementation, are presented below and summarized in Table 54.

To prevent dependency on national treasuries' resources, both treaties provide for the creation of an autonomous community budget, with earmarked tax and customs resources, and annual budgeting procedures to fix both the recurrent expenditures of the new institutions and regional economic interventions, notably in the area of sectoral policies.

Toward a Common Market

Both subregions have set the goal of a common market for their member countries, involving a free flow of goods, services, persons, and capital. Meeting this goal requires: (a) the establishment of a full-

[1]As of September 1995.

[2]Accordingly, the Economic Community of West Africa (CEAO), which included all WAMU member countries but Togo, and included Mauritania as well, was dissolved; in Central Africa, the CAEMC will succeed the Central African Monetary Area (CAMA) and the Central African Economic and Customs Union (CAECU).

Table 54. Summary of Economic Integration Initiatives/Results in the CFA Franc Zone

	West African Economic and Monetary Union		Central African Economic and Monetary Community	
Project	Content	Implementation	Content	Implementation
Institutional Arrangements				
Treaty establishing the economic union	• Enlarges the monetary union to economic integration, defines the new institutions, and the scope of their activities.	Signed on January 10, 1994; effective on August 1, 1994.	• Umbrella treaty for both economic and monetary unions.	Signed on March 16, 1994; specific conventions on both monetary and economic unions still under negotiation.
Executive authority	• Creates a seven-member executive committee (the Commission).	Installed January 30, 1995 in Ouagadougou.	• Creates an Executive Secretariat (to replace the CAECU General Secretariat).	Draft proposal.
Judiciary authority	• Creates a Court of Justice.	Installed January 30, 1995.	• Creates a Court of Justice.	Draft proposal.
Community budget	• Earmarks tax and customs resources to finance recurrent and intervention expenditures.	Autonomous budget to be put in place by 1997. Transitory period financed by the BCEAO and the BOAD.	• Earmarks tax and customs resources to finance recurrent expenditures.	Not specified.
Common market				
Customs union	• Common external tariff (may consist of three rates); preferential rate for intraregional trade to be phased out progressively; elimination of nontariff barriers within the union; and harmonization of tax regimes, including exemptions.	Preliminary proposals on the general principles based on three specific studies. However, differences in customs tariff rates have already been reduced in the context of the CFA franc devaluation.	• Common external tariff consisting of four rates (5, 10, 20, and 30 percent), and a preferential tariff for intraregional trade (20 percent of the CET, to be phased out by 1998).	Partly implemented in 1994 and in full by mid-1995, temporary surtaxes (30 percent maximum) allowed on a limited list of products.
			• Elimination of ad hoc exemptions.	Unevenly implemented in 1994.
			• Elimination of exemptions included in bilateral agreements between governments and companies.	To be completed by end-1995.
Tax harmonization				
Indirect taxes	• VAT with a limited number of rates and of exemptions.	Significant progress toward harmonization in 1994–95 through measures included in programs supported by the use of Fund resources.	• Turnover tax consisting of two rates, with a normal rate in the 7–18 percent range, and a reduced rate in the 3–6 percent range.	Implemented in 1994, except in Gabon, which introduced a single-rate VAT system in April 1995.
	• Common list of excisable goods.	Being studied.	• Common list of excisable goods.	Implemented in 1994 .
Regional financial market	• Creation of a regional stock market.	Mid-1996, will replace the present stock market in Abidjan.		

Table 54 *(concluded)*

Project	West African Economic and Monetary Union		Central African Economic and Monetary Community	
	Content	Implementation	Content	Implementation
Regulatory framework	• Harmonization of technical norms.	Not started.		
	• Free intraregional competition to be achieved by forbidding restrictive practices, including government intervention.	Not started.		
	• Common investment code.	Preliminary study by the BCEAO.	• Adaptation of national investment codes to the common tax and customs regime.	Achieved in all countries but the C.A.R. and Chad.
Surveillance of fiscal policies				
Fiscal indicators	• List of five quantitative fiscal indicators centering on primary surplus, domestic and external arrears, wage bill, and investment financed by domestic resources.	Adopted in September 1993.	• List of four fiscal norms centering on the primary surplus, domestic and external arrears, and wage bill. In addition, use of present national foreign reserves indicators as a possible sign of excessive public sector bank borrowing.	Still to be adopted.
Surveillance procedures	• Periodic reports by the Commission, including recommendations to countries not satisfying the norms.	In 1994, the BCEAO submitted a quarterly report to the Council of Ministers, which presented each country's position with respect to the five indicators. Should be taken over in 1995 by the Commission itself.	• A regional surveillance committee will prepare semiannual reports to the Council of Ministers.	Still to be adopted.
Sanctions	• Provided for in the Treaty, the first step being the publication of a report by the Commission.	In process.	• Limited to the publication of a communiqué mentioning noncompliance with indicators.	Still to be adopted.
Budget law and public accounting, public finance, and price statistics	• Harmonization.	Studies being prepared with technical assistance from the French CFD, the Fund, and the European Union.		
Sectoral policies				
Human resources	• Education, research, vocational training.	Studies being prepared by the BOAD.	• Common policies in education, research, vocational training.	Implementation should start within the first five years following treaty ratification.
Regional development	• To open up landlocked areas.	Studies being prepared by the BOAD.		
Other areas	• Including agricultural, energy, manufacturing industry, environment, and transportation.	Studies being prepared by the BOAD.	• Harmonization of policies in other sectors, including agriculture, energy, manufacturing environment, and transportation.	

fledged customs union based on a free trade area—that is, the elimination of tariff and nontariff barriers within the subregion—protected by a common external tariff (CET); (b) the harmonization of domestic tax regimes, notably for indirect taxation; and (c) the definition of a common regulatory framework in a number of areas such as technical norms, financial transactions, and government subsidies.

In the WAEMU region, discussions on the CET are still at a preliminary stage. A possible option, which was considered by the Steering Committee in May 1994, based on a preliminary study financed by a bilateral donor, could include inter alia a three-tier tariff and an intraregional tariff.[3] However, the implications of these proposals for the members' public finances are still to be assessed, and an agenda defining the sequence of steps leading to the CET must be drawn up. The objective of narrowing national discrepancies between indirect tax regimes was retained as a condition for establishing a true regional common market, and also with a view to rationalizing and simplifying existing tax systems. Based on preliminary studies, the Steering Committee recommended the adoption in each member country of a value-added tax (VAT) with at most two rates.

In the CAEMC, the customs union has, by and large, already been implemented in the context of the CAECU-sponsored tax and customs reform launched in Bangui in June 1993, and guided by a Steering Committee including donors. The provisions of the reform included (a) a four-tier CET (at rates of 5, 15, 35, and 50 percent); (b) a preferential tariff rate for intraregional trade, set initially at 20 percent of CET, to be phased out gradually by January 1, 1998; (c) a turnover tax (TCA) with two rates—a normal rate in the 7–18 percent range, and a reduced rate in the 3–6 percent range to replace the existing domestic production and sales taxes, and to be replaced in turn in due course by a VAT;[4] (d) excise taxes and temporary surtaxes on a limited list of products; and (e) the elimination of all customs and indirect tax exemptions, including those attached to current investment codes or to special regimes.[5]

[3]This intraregional tariff would replace the regional cooperation tax (TCR) that was eliminated de facto in 1994 with the decision to dissolve the CEAO. Following this dissolution, some countries decided to abolish the regional preferential treatment by submitting regional trade to their own external tariff in March 1994. Because of the damage thus caused to a few member countries, a new regime for intraregional flows is being prepared presently by the WAEMU Commission.

[4]With the exception of Gabon, which moved immediately to a VAT on April 1, 1995.

[5]Notably, by renegotiating the tax incentives provided for in bilateral agreements between governments and companies (conventions d'établissement).

Progress in the harmonization of customs tariffs and indirect taxes in both unions over 1993–95 is summarized in Table 55. Although reforms are being prepared slowly in the WAEMU, the adoption in 1994 of Fund-supported adjustment programs by the seven member countries led to a significant narrowing of customs tariff and tax rates dispersion. In particular, the three countries (Côte d'Ivoire, Niger, and Senegal) that had a VAT with three rates or more in 1993 reduced these rates to two or fewer in 1994–95. Togo introduced a VAT with two rates on July 1, 1995.

CAECU member countries took most of the planned measures in the aftermath of the CFA franc devaluation in 1994, although they decided to lower the CET rates to 5, 10, 20, and 30 percent, respectively, to alleviate the increase in the cost of imports. By the end of 1994, the common external and preferential tariffs, as well as the turnover and excise taxes, had been implemented in all countries but Chad (where only the CET and temporary surtaxes had been implemented). Chad, however, implemented the remainder of the reform effective July 1, 1995.

In practice, the broadening of the tax base predicated on these reforms did not occur at the speed or on the scale that had been expected, as exemptions—whether granted on an ad hoc basis, or attached to investment codes or special regimes—were not fully eliminated (although the investment codes of Cameroon and Gabon were duly adjusted). The CAECU member countries also resorted temporarily to safeguard measures with a view to limiting the price increases of essential commodities in the aftermath of the devaluation; these measures included partial or total exemptions of customs duties and turnover tax (Cameroon, Central African Republic, Chad) or the declassification of some imports from the two highest tariff categories to the lowest one (Congo, Equatorial Guinea). In order to restore the momentum of implementation of the CAECU reform, as envisaged in the Bangui agreement, the Steering Committee urged member countries during its meeting in Malabo in April 1995 (a) to draw up a list of observed deficiencies and eliminate them by end-June 1995; (b) to prepare a comprehensive inventory of all remaining ad hoc or regulatory tax exemptions and abolish those that are not supported by international treaties by end-June 1995; and (c) to proceed without further delay (by the end of December 1995 at the latest), with the elimination of tax exemptions provided for in bilateral agreements with companies.

Regional Surveillance

As included in the WAEMU treaty and as envisaged in the CAEU convention, the regional surveillance of economic policies within both unions is in-

Table 55. Harmonization of Customs Duties and Indirect Taxes in the CFA Franc Zone
(In percent unless otherwise specified)

	West African Economic and Monetary Union							Central African Economic and Monetary Community					
	Benin	Burkina Faso	Côte d'Ivoire	Mali	Niger	Senegal	Togo	Cameroon	C.A.R.	Chad	Congo	Equatorial Guinea	Gabon
Status in 1993													
Customs tariff rates[1,2]	0–160	0–33	0–151	0–36	0–66	0–65	0–30	0–285	0–190	0–155	0–40	2.5–305	0–260
Statistical fee rate	3	4	2.5	3–5	4.5	6–12	3	—	1	1	0.2	—	2
Turnover tax rates	—	—	—	—	—	—	—	2.25–305	2.4–16.5	15	0.5–13.6	10	5–14
Value-added tax (VAT) rates	18	10–15	5–35	10–17	10–24	7–34	5–30	—	—	—	—	—	—
Total taxation[3]	21.5–216	14–52	7.6–217	3–65	15–115	12–127	8.2–74	2.25–305	3.4–207	16–170	0.7–159	12.8–346	7–276
Number of customs tariff rates	12	7	. . .	. . .	. . .	5	5	. . .	. . .	. . .	. . .	. . .	. . .
Existence of nontariff barriers (Yes/No)	No	Yes	Yes	No	Yes	Yes	Yes	Yes	Yes	Yes	Yes	No	Yes
Exemptions from customs duties (in percent of imports)	27	. . .	22	23	44	28	22	58	61	. . .	58	65	44
Number of turnover tax/VAT rates[4]	1	1	5	2	3	5	3	8	7	1	4	1	5
Excise duties and other indirect taxes[5]	P,A,T,O	P,A,T,O	P,A,T,O	P,A,T,O	P,A,T,O	A,T,O	A,T,O	P,A,T,O	P,O	P,A,T,O	P,A	P,A,T,O	P,A,T,O
Status as of September 1995													
Customs tariff rates[1,6]	0–20	0–33	0–35	0–30	0–30	0–40	0–20	5–30	5–30	5–30	5–30	5–30	5–30
Statistical fee rate	5	4	2.5	3–5	5	5	3	—	1	1	1	—	2
Turnover tax rates	—	—	—	—	—	—	—	8–17	5–16	5–15	5–15	5–12	—
Value-added tax (VAT) rates	18	15	11–20	10–15	17	10–20	7–18	—	—	—	—	—	18
Total taxation[3]	23.9–49	19–52	13.8–65	3–55	22.9–59.7	5–73	10.2–46	13.4–52.1	11.3–52	11.3–50.7	11.3–50.7	10.3–45.6	7–55
Number of customs tariff rates	5	7	8	5	3	4	4	4	4	4	4	4	4
Elimination of nontariff barriers[7]	T	P,R	P	T	T	P,R	P	T,R	T,R	T,R	T,R	—	P,R
Exemptions from customs duties (in percent of imports)	. . .	. . .	. . .	. . .	. . .	. . .	. . .	39	66	. . .	46	65	33
Number of turnover tax/VAT rates[4]	1	1	2	2	1	2	2	2	2	2	2	2	1
Excise duties and other indirect taxes[5]	P,A,T,O	P,A,T,O	P,A,T,O	P,A,T,O	P,A,T,O	A,T,O	A,T,O	P,A,T,O	P,A,T,O	P,A,T,O	P,A,T,O	P,A,T,O	P,A,T,O

Source: Data provided by the authorities.
[1]Consolidated customs and fiscal import duties. Excluding statistical fees and temporary surcharges.
[2]In the WAEMU, intraregional trade flows of CEAO countries were subject to a preferential rate (TCR).
[3]Excluding excise duties.
[4]Excluding the zero rate for exports.
[5]Petroleum products (P), alcoholic beverages (A), tobacco (T), other (O).
[6]In the WAEMU, following the dissolution of the CEAO, the TCR was abolished. In the CAEMC, a generalized preferential rate for intraregional trade is applied at 20 percent of the standard common external tariff, to be reduced to 10 percent on January 1, 1996, and eliminated on January 1, 1998.
[7]Total elimination (T), Partial elimination (P), Replacement by temporary surcharges (R).

tended to prevent member countries from incurring excessive government deficits or from adopting inappropriate expenditure structures, as well as fiscal policy stances inconsistent with the commonly defined monetary policy objectives.[6] The surveillance procedure is based on the common review of selected fiscal "convergence indicators" focusing on primary balances, wage bills, and domestic and external arrears. For WAEMU countries, it also includes the share of public resources devoted to public investment; and for each indicator, nonbinding quantitative norms have been agreed.[7] For CAEMC countries, primary balances are expected to be positive, changes in the wage bill should be equal or less than change in government revenue, and domestic and external payments arrears should not be accumulated; in addition, the fiscal stance is explicitly supposed to be adjusted whenever the country's contribution to the level of foreign reserves of the BEAC falls below the common norm.[8] In both unions, the surveillance mechanism is expected to be complemented: (a) upstream, by efforts to harmonize public finance statistics, as well as budget laws and procedures; and (b) downstream, by mechanisms allowing public disclosure of recommendations and eventually, at least in the WAEMU, by sanctions vis-à-vis those countries that maintain inappropriate policies.

In the WAEMU, the set of convergence indicators was adopted in September 1993 after consultations with the Fund and other donors. While recognizing that any reliance on these indicators would represent, in the present situation, an important contribution to the strengthening of public sector financial positions, the Fund staff cautioned against adopting too rigid an approach in defining excessive deficits and inappropriate public expenditure structures. It encouraged a further elaboration of fiscal norms based on more country-specific approaches, taking into account the level of public debt, the sustainability of public deficits, and the likelihood of different cyclical developments between countries. The Fund staff also pointed to the varying vulnerability of WAEMU countries to terms of trade and other shocks, and to the need for room to maneuver should one or several countries be buffeted by such temporary shocks. There would also be a need in such circumstances for some coordination and assistance at the regional level. Since September 1993, fiscal surveillance, including the review of these indicators, has been conducted on a quarterly basis by the Council of Ministers of the WAEMU; it has now been taken over by the newly installed Commission.

In the CAEMC countries, the surveillance mechanism is still not in place, but its broad principles in the draft CAEU convention are roughly similar. The prudence suggested by the Fund staff has, if anything, been even greater in this case because of the considerable differences in endowment, stages of development, and prospects for fiscal and external viability in the CAEMC countries (for instance, Gabon's per capita income is about 12 times that of Chad).

Sectoral Policies

Both unions place a high priority on the coordination of the sectoral policies implemented by the member countries, and, for the long run, envisage adopting common and complementary policies in a large number of areas, including human resource development, agriculture, industry, transportation, and the environment. Education, research, and vocational training have been identified as areas where common actions could be taken rapidly, so as to achieve economies of scale in budgetary programs and improve the free circulation of skilled labor within the unions by harmonizing diplomas. The WAEMU treaty foresees the implementation of regional development policies, including the harmonization of national infrastructure programs, and opening up landlocked areas. These policies could be financed by resources of the common budget through structural funds that would have to be established.

So far, no sectoral initiatives have started in either union. In the WAEMU, however, the West African Development Bank has been entrusted with the task of undertaking studies and making proposals to the Council of Ministers.

Zone-Wide Initiatives

In parallel with these initiatives in the two subregions, several important initiatives are also being pursued at the level of the CFA franc zone as a whole (Table 56). The key objectives are (a) harmonizing the legal and regulatory framework in critical areas; and (b) creating common institutions that oversee and ensure the implementation of regional

[6]As a transitional measure, Convergence Councils (Conseils de Convergence) were created as early as September 1992 in both subregions under the joint chairmanship of the respective common central bank and the French Treasury. The committees' principal tasks were to review the implementation of the adjustment programs in member countries, particularly in the fiscal area.

[7]Three norms are defined in terms of fiscal revenue: the wage bill should not exceed 50 percent, the primary surplus should stay above 15 percent, and public investment financed by domestic resources should be at least 20 percent. The other two norms relate to the nonaccumulation of domestic and external arrears.

[8]This norm is defined in the BEAC's statutes and requires that foreign exchange reserves of each member country cover at least 20 percent of the short-term liabilities of the BEAC's national agency.

Table 56. Economic Integration Projects at the CFA Franc Zone Level

Project	Content	Implementation
Business law	• General treaty establishing the Organization for the Harmonization of Business Law in Africa (OHADA) and related institutions.	Signed on October 17, 1993, by the 14 franc zone countries plus Guinea-Bissau, already ratified by 10 countries. Open to all OAU countries.
	• Harmonization of commercial law, corporate law, private accounting laws and plans, bankruptcy and debt recovery procedures, and securities law. Could be extended to other fields, including labor codes.	To be completed by March 1996.
	• Creation of a regional Court of Justice to ensure the judicial enforcement of the uniform laws.	To be effective in mid-1996.
	• Creation of a common training institute	
Insurance sector	• General treaty establishing the Interafrican Conference of Insurance Markets (CIMA), and related institutions.	Signed on July 10, 1992; ratified by the 14 franc zone countries.
	• Common insurance code regulating insurance companies.	Effective February 1, 1995.
	• Regional insurance commission, in charge of regulatory and prudential supervision, as well as of granting and withdrawing licenses.	Based in Libreville (Gabon), effective by September 1995.
Social Security institutions	• General treaty establishing the Interafrican Conference of Social Security Funds (CIPRES) and related institutions.	Signed on September 21, 1993, ratified by six countries, not effective yet.
	• Common regulatory, accounting, and financial framework.	
	• Regional Commission, notably in charge of regular financial audits of Social Security Funds.	To be based in Libreville (Gabon).
Statistics	• General treaty establishing an African Institute of Statistics (AFRISTAT), in charge of defining common concepts and methodologies, producing studies, supporting national institutes, and providing training to civil servants of member countries institutions.	Signed on September 21, 1993, ratified by six countries, not effective yet. To be based in Bamako (Mali).

regulations. These objectives have already been achieved in both subregions for the banking sector where, following the creation of independent regional banking commissions, common regulatory standards have been established (see Annex III). A single and updated insurance code also came into force in the zone on February 1, 1995; and, in the course of the next few months, a regional supervisory agency is to take over from the national administrations the supervision of insurance companies.[9] In a similar vein, a regional supervisory agency responsible for the technical and financial audits of individual countries' social security institutions is to be set up in the course of 1996.[10] In addition, a regional institution (AFRISTAT) has been established, to provide common methodologies and facilities in the statistical area.

Among these zone-wide initiatives, the ongoing project on harmonization of business law is possibly the most ambitious. The Organization for the Harmonization of Business Law in Africa (OHADA) is intended to establish a set of uniform laws covering the main areas of business law, as well as a regional Court of Justice that will ensure the judicial enforcement of the laws. OHADA's objective is to provide for a sound, stable, and predictable environment conducive to sustained private sector development. Thirteen CFA franc countries, as well as Comoros and Guinea-Bissau, signed the treaty establishing the OHADA in October 1993—which has come into force in September 1995, following the ratification by eleven countries (Benin, Burkina Faso, Cameroon, the Central African Republic, the Comoros, Côte d'Ivoire, Guinea-Bissau, Mali, Niger, Senegal, and Togo). The minimum number of ratifications required by the treaty has

[9]The insurance commission of the Interafrican Conference of Insurance Markets (CIMA) will be based in Libreville.

[10]The treaty establishing the Interafrican Conference for Social Security Funds (CIPRES) had been ratified by eight governments at the end of September 1995 and has thus entered into force. Moreover, the agency's statutes and the prudential regulations to be enforced by social security institutions have already been finalized.

thus been reached. The areas of business law that most urgently need to be harmonized include notably corporate and commercial law; harmonized regulations are currently being reviewed by national commissions and should be finalized by March 1996. Accordingly, the regional institutions, including the Court of Justice, should become operational in 1996.[11]

[11]Even in the case of failure of the OHADA initiative, a readily available set of uniform laws could prove helpful in some countries where most business regulations are considered to be obsolete.

Annex III Monetary Policy and Banking Supervision in the Two Unions of the CFA Franc Zone

Monetary policy in the CFA franc zone is governed by the regional monetary arrangements in force within the WAEMU and CAEMC. Both unions have a common currency—the CFA franc—that is pegged to the French franc. Each union has a regional central bank (with agencies at the national level), which holds the pooled foreign reserves of the union, and conducts monetary policy at the regional level.[1]

Because of the fixed exchange rate and the substantial degree of capital mobility and substitutability that generally prevails between France and the unions, the room for an independent monetary policy at the level of the two subregions is limited.[2] Monetary policy instruments therefore serve principally to maintain the desired distribution between the central banks' domestic and foreign assets. In addition, the substitution in 1993–94 of indirect monetary policy instruments for country and bank-specific credit ceilings, and the ongoing development of regional/interbank and money markets, have largely eliminated the room for country-specific monetary policies.

This regional dimension of monetary arrangements and policies has also carried over into the area of banking regulations and supervision. In particular, common supervisory bodies have been established, and common banking regulations adopted, by each of the two unions in the aftermath of the economic crisis of the late 1980s–early 1990s and the resulting collapse of a number of banking institutions.

Given this regional dimension of the problems facing the CFA franc zone and of the policies and solutions that have been developed over the years, bilateral discussions between Fund staff and the BCEAO and the BEAC have been held approximately on a semiannual basis since 1990. The last two rounds of discussions took place in February 1995 with the BEAC and March 1995 with the BCEAO.

[1]As of June 1995.

[2]The principles of the fixed exchange rate and of free capital transferability are set out in the cooperation treaties between France and the two monetary unions.

Reforms of Monetary Policy Instruments

Until the early 1990s, monetary policy in both unions relied by and large on direct instruments. Lending and deposit rates were fixed administratively by the central banks. Credit ceilings were set for each country and for each type of credit, and were then translated into ceilings for individual banks, as well as for large individual borrowers. The statutes of the two central banks guaranteed national treasuries an overdraft facility (known as statutory advances), which was limited in principle to 20 percent of the previous year's domestic tax revenue in the respective countries. Preferential interest rates were applied to certain central bank credits, notably to crop credit refinancing (which was also excluded from the national credit ceilings) and to the statutory advances. For any loan operation to be eligible for central bank refinancing, commercial banks had to obtain prior authorization from the monetary authority.

As part of the efforts undertaken in the late 1980s and early 1990s to overcome member countries' economic and financial difficulties, and to rely more systematically on market forces to reduce distortions, monetary reforms aimed at replacing direct instruments with indirect instruments of monetary policy were launched in both unions at the end of the 1980s (Table 57). These reforms were implemented in two stages.

During 1989–92, credit controls and selective interest rates were abolished progressively. In the WAEMU, crop credit was brought under the national overall credit ceiling, and in 1992 the prior approval requirement for individual loans was replaced by a new creditworthiness rating system to govern overall central bank refinancing policy. In both unions, discount rates were unified. In the CAEMC, a timetable was established for stepwise increases in

Table 57. Status of Monetary Reforms in the Two Unions of the CFA Franc Zone

	West African Economic and Monetary Union		Central African Economic and Monetary Community	
	Content	Implementation, comments	Content	Implementation, comments
Money market				
Auctions of loanable funds	Weekly, organized at the regional level, open to the zone's banks, financial institutions, and, to a limited extent, to Treasuries. The central bank is the sole counterpart of transactions; bids have to be backed by admissible commercial paper. The central bank may offer credit, or bid for liquidity, according to its monetary targets.	Effective October 1993. The central bank has not absorbed excess liquidity through auctions.	Weekly, organized at the level of national agencies.	Effective July 1994. Interventions are limited by country-specific refinancing ceilings. Special deposits are the only mechanism for absorbing excess bank liquidity (see below).
Alternative interventions	• Repurchase agreements of commercial paper.	Rarely used at present.	• Repurchase agreements with commercial banks, two-to-seven day maturities.	Effective July 1994.
	• Discount.	Rarely used at present.	• Penalty rate.	
			• Automatic refinancing (B window) for medium-term credit to "productive sectors."	Not included in the refinancing ceiling.
Interbank interventions	No intervention.	Regional interbank market.	Exceptional day-to-day interventions when the refinancing ceilings are reached.	Regional interbank market.
Advances to the Treasury	Limited to 20 percent of domestic tax receipts of the previous year.	Penalty rates are applied to advances above the ceiling.	Limited to 20 percent of domestic revenue of the previous year.	Penalty rates are applied to advances above the ceiling.
Reserves				
Minimum reserve requirements	1.5 percent of the sum of sight deposits and short-term credit, excluding crop credit.	Effective December 1993. Reserves are not remunerated.	In percentage of sight, time, and savings deposits.	Not activated yet.
Free reserves	Not remunerated.	Alternatively, commercial banks can use their excess liquidity to buy securitized BCEAO claims to the government at a fixed rate. These securities are redeemable at par at any time, without restrictions.	Commercial banks can deposit their excess liquidity in remunerated accounts with the central bank (special deposits).	
Interest rates				
Deposits	Free, except a minimum rate on passbook savings deposits.	Sight deposits cannot be remunerated.	Minimum fixed by the central bank.	
Lending	Free, except a maximum lending rate (usurious, set at twice the discount rate).		Maximum rate fixed by the central bank.	
Refinancing	• Auction rate.	Set by the central bank.	• Auction rate.	Set by the central bank.
	• Repurchase agreement rate, fixed by the central bank.	Set by the central bank about 100–250 basis points above the auction rate.	• Repurchase agreement rate.	Set by the central bank 150–200 basis points above the auction rate.
	• Discount rate, fixed by the central bank.	Set by the central bank. Penalty rate.	• Penalty rate.	Set by the central bank.
			• Special refinancing rate (B window).	For credits allowed after July 1994, fixed to the average auction rate over the last six months.
	• Interbank rate.	Freely negotiated.	• Interbank rate.	Freely negotiated.

the rate applied to advances to governments, up to the level of the standard discount rate.[3]

Beginning in October 1993 in the WAEMU, and in July 1994 in the CAEMC, the central banks moved decisively to a system of monetary management based on indirect instruments of monetary policy operating in the context of regional interbank and money markets. These instruments have consisted principally of money market auctions and minimum reserve requirements (the latter in place only in the WAEMU). In the WAEMU, the central bank also proceeded with the liberalization of interest rates.

In both unions, the new money market auctions are open to the banks and financial institutions of the union and are conducted on a weekly basis. In the WAEMU, the auction is organized at the regional level; banks submit to the central bank weekly offers of, or bids for, loanable funds in tranches, with a specified interest rate for each; the BCEAO can intervene, either on the demand or on the supply side, in accordance with its regional targets for credit aggregates; and supply or demand may be rationed and satisfied on a prorated basis. In the CAEMC, in contrast, the auction is organized at the level of the national agencies; it consists only of central bank credit on offer for an amount limited by country-specific ceilings, and the BEAC satisfies bank demands on a prorated basis. In both unions, the central bank determines the interest rate at which transactions are settled. In addition to the auctions, the discount window—the discount rate in the WAEMU, and the penalty rate in the CAEMC—remains in place. The BCEAO and the BEAC have also introduced repurchase agreements (prises en pension) to provide temporary liquidity to banks at a rate between the discount rate and the money market rate.[4] A special window also remains open at the BEAC, which allows banks to refinance automatically medium-term credits to the so-called productive sectors outside the national refinancing ceiling.[5]

These reforms have been paralleled by the emergence of interbank markets at the regional level, where interest rates are freely negotiated and where operations are conducted without the intervention of the central banks. Once these markets have developed more fully and have acquired the necessary depth, expectations are that the central banks will substitute the current auction mechanism by interventions at the margin in these markets, so as to mop up or inject liquidity.

Legal reserve requirements are available as an instrument in both unions. In the WAEMU, the minimum reserve requirement has been set at 1.5 percent of the sum of sight deposits and short-term credits (excluding crop credits).[6] Admissible reserves are non-interest-bearing deposits held at the central bank, as well as certain government securities (see below). Excess reserves are not remunerated. Legal reserve requirements have also been provided for in the CAEMC, but have not been activated. Unlike the BCEAO, however, the BEAC remunerates commercial banks' free reserves ("special deposits") at a rate that it sets periodically (currently 4½ percent). These special deposits are thus akin in their effect to open market (absorption) operations, except for the fact that the prevailing interest rate is probably well above market-clearing levels.

In addition to these reforms, the BCEAO has liberalized commercial bank interest rates, except the usurious lending rate (which is set at twice the discount rate) and the minimum rate on passbook savings deposits.[7] In contrast, the BEAC continues to set maximum lending and minimum deposit rates, all of which are similar across the CAEMC except the rates on passbook savings.[8]

Recent Developments in Money Markets

Activity in the money and interbank markets has remained modest so far in both unions, reflecting mainly banks' comfortable liquidity and a certain re-

[3]Unification was eventually achieved in June 1994. The rates have diverged again since March 1995, however, when the auction rate was raised from 7.75 percent to 8.0 percent, and the rate on government advances remained unchanged. In the WAEMU, advances to governments have continued to benefit from a preferential interest rate. In both unions, the penalty rate on advances exceeding the statutory ceiling has always remained below the penalty rate applicable to banks.

[4]The BEAC may also resort to exceptional day-to-day interventions in the interbank market at discretionary rates (though at a rate higher than that of the repurchase agreements) when the refinancing ceiling in an individual country is exceeded.

[5]The rate applicable to this special rediscount facility is adjusted twice a year on the basis of the average auction rate during the previous six-month period.

[6]The minimum reserve requirement is presently set at a uniform rate for all WAEMU member countries, although the central bank is empowered in principle to set country-specific rates.

[7]Moreover, the interest rates payable on time deposits and on certificates of deposit (bons de caisse), with a maturity of less than one year and in amounts below a ceiling set by the central bank, are now automatically adjusted in line with changes in the money market rate.

[8]However, in accordance with a decision of its Executive Board of July 1995, the BEAC is expected by January 1996 to eliminate the minimum deposit rates (except for passbook savings), while the maximum lending rates will be set at a margin above the penalty rate, that is, close to the level of the usurious rate in the WAEMU.

luctance on the part of the two central banks to absorb excess bank loanable funds because of the attendant costs. A significant bank risk in a few countries has also contributed to the slow development of the market in the CAEMC.

WAEMU

Since the introduction of the money market in October 1993, the central bank has limited its intervention mostly to intermediating between banks with excess liquidity and banks with financing needs (mainly Ivoirian banks), with limited net intervention in auctions or reverse auctions of central bank money. From October 1993 to late February 1994, the BCEAO absorptions were in the range of CFAF 20–40 billion—at a fixed rate of 5 percent—leaving an excess of funds in the market reaching up to CFAF 190 billion, which remained as unremunerated excess reserves with the central bank. Yet, however modest, these absorption operations were discontinued in late February 1994. As the year advanced and financing needs in the union remained generally slack, it became even more difficult for banks with excess funds to find counterparts in the market. Thus, while 36 percent of funds on offer still found takers in the first five months of the year, this proportion declined to 2 percent in the third quarter, recovering only slightly to 6 percent in the fourth quarter. The central bank accordingly lowered its intervention rate at the auction, from 9.25 percent in the first five months of 1994 to 5.5 percent in September, where it remained thereafter. During that period, discount and repurchase agreement operations were few and far between.

Given these growing difficulties in placing excess liquidity in the money market, banks have become more active in trying to place funds with other banks through the interbank market. Operations in that market increased markedly in late 1994 with the beginning of the crop season, notably in Côte d'Ivoire, where large amounts are required for coffee and cocoa prefinancing.[9]

To mop up part of the large liquidity, in mid-1994 the BCEAO decided to securitize and sell the consolidated claims it had held on governments on account of the restructuring of the banking systems of the union in the late 1980s. The total claims that could be securitized under this scheme were equivalent to some CFAF 440 billion, or 17 percent of broad money in the WAEMU at end-1994, and carried an original maturity of 15 years, with 3 years' grace.[10] While the initial BCEAO claims bore interest at 3 percent, to be paid by the governments, the interest rate on the bonds issued in the context of the securitization has been set at 5 percent, tax free, with the difference being paid by the central bank. The bonds are offered to commercial banks and other financial institutions in the union, and they can be used to meet legal reserve requirements. As the initial reaction of banks to the scheme was muted, the BCEAO decided in September 1994 to make the bonds more attractive by allowing for their redemption at par and at any time, without any restriction by the central bank. Placements accelerated substantially after the introduction of this provision. At end-March 1995, 75 percent of member country governments' consolidated debts had been placed; however, banks' excess reserves with the BCEAO still amounted to more than CFAF 110 billion.

CAEMC

Central bank injection of liquidity was modest in 1994, and was driven more by the BEAC's role as a lender of last resort to weak institutions than by demand management considerations.

Cameroon was by and large the most active taker at the BEAC auction, with central bank refinancing to Cameroonian banks accounting on average for 90 percent of the BEAC's zone-wide interventions. At 8.0 percent (8.75 percent since June 29, 1995), the interest rate in the BEAC auction market remained significantly above the French rate, reflecting central bank concerns over the weakening of its foreign reserve position.

Activity in the regional interbank market has also remained modest. Most transactions have taken place within the same banking group or have taken the form of one-way lending to Gabonese banks. Interbank transactions rates have thus tended to fluctuate strongly, although in the last few months rates have remained within the range between the auction rates and the special deposits rate, as would normally be expected.

Given this slow start in interbank lending and the increase in bank liquidity in 1994, commercial banks first repaid their earlier recourse to central bank rediscounts. The banks also built up sizable reserves with the BEAC (CFAF 91 billion at end-March

---

[9]The weekly average transactions in the interbank market amounted to CFAF 22.8 billion during the last quarter of 1994, almost twice the level of transactions in the auction (money) market.

[10]Securities were to be distributed as follows: claims on the government of Benin, CFAF 44.3 billion; of Burkina Faso, CFAF 9 billion; of Côte d'Ivoire, CFAF 186.1 billion; of Mali, CFAF 23.9 billion; of Niger, CFAF 25.9 billion; of Senegal, CFAF 143.7 billion; and of Togo, CFAF 7.5 billion. The bonds issued have a maturity corresponding to the remaining duration of the claims; if all were issued on January 1, 1994, the average maturity of the bonds would have been 12.5 years, with six months' grace.

1995), mostly in the form of special deposits, despite reductions in the remuneration rate from 9.75 percent in January 1994 to 4.2 percent in March 1995 (4.5 percent since end-June).

Need for Additional Reforms

As the discussion above indicates, the transition to fully functioning indirect instruments of monetary management is incomplete and a number of weaknesses need remedying.

Certain features in each union undermine the ability of the market to play its role, and of the monetary authorities to achieve their objectives. First, the administrative determination by the central banks of both prices and quantities in their intervention in the money market prevents the emergence of a market-clearing interest rate and introduces a distortion in the rate structure. Second, this distortion is aggravated in the WAEMU by the lack of central bank remuneration of excess reserves at a time when domestic credit demand is slack. Third, in case of a recovery in private sector credit demand, the two central banks do not appear to be equipped with the instruments needed to maintain control over the composition of their net assets. In particular, the readiness of the BCEAO to redeem the bonds issued under the securitization scheme at par and at any time, the highly liquid character of the special deposits maintained with the BEAC, and the open-ended possibility of refinancing medium-term credit to productive sectors at the BEAC all undermine the two central banks' ability to maintain control over their own domestic assets. Fourth, it seems to be contrary to the intent of legal reserve requirements to allow bonds acquired under the securitization scheme to be used in the discharge of required reserves. Finally, the design of legal reserve requirements in the WAEMU, which incorporates short-term loans in the basis of the calculation for the required reserves, reintroduces de facto an element of selective credit allocation.

To address these weaknesses, policy instruments need to be improved and made symmetrical. In particular, the central banks should begin issuing their own debt instruments to serve initially as a support for auctions or reverse auctions in the money market, and then influence the interbank market at the margin once it has acquired sufficient depth while allowing interest rates to clear the markets. In this context, it appears that the modalities of the securitization scheme in the WAEMU and of the special deposits scheme at the BEAC would need to be reviewed.

These and other issues have been taken up in the course of the most recent discussions with the two central banks. As noted earlier, the BEAC took some corrective action at its July 1995 Board meeting. Reverse auction mechanisms are to be introduced (including the elimination of special deposits), and the administrative determination of banks' minimum deposit and maximum lending rates is to be relaxed, with effect from January 1996. Much remains to be done, however, if the full benefits of relying on market mechanisms are to be realized. Action must also be taken to strengthen the health of the banking systems of the union, particularly in the CAEMC, for market-based instruments are of little help where the financial institutions themselves are thought to pose a risk.

Implications for Monetary Programming

Both unions follow at present a cycle of semiannual monetary programming, with broad objectives set at the regional level and detailed programming at the national level to ensure compatibility with these regional objectives. Monetary programming relies on the setting of regional objectives for external reserves, taking into account regional balance of payments projections and the need to maintain (or restore) the 20 percent statutory foreign exchange cover requirement for the central banks' short-term liabilities. On this basis, credit objectives are established for each individual country, including national refinancing ceilings in the CAEMC.

The reform of policy instrumentation since 1993–94 has had two important implications for monetary programming: (a) with the elimination of the system of credit ceilings, attainment of the external reserve objectives has to rely exclusively on central bank interventions through the banks' various refinancing and absorption facilities; and (b) central banks may affect the behavior of bank credit only at the regional level, since the development of regional money and interbank markets would lead to a rapid redistribution of loanable funds throughout the zone, should an attempt be made to enforce national targets. Accordingly, for purposes of programs supported by the Fund, country-specific objectives for credit to the private sector have become of limited use, and the government's domestic borrowing requirement, as proxied by net bank credit to government, has become in practice the only immediate instrument to influence individual country contributions to the respective net foreign positions of the two central banks.[11] It is

[11]The central relevance of net bank credit to government as an instrument to achieve national targets consistent with regional net foreign asset objectives is explicitly noted in the fiscal surveillance mechanism elaborated in the draft convention establishing an economic union within the CAEMC (see Annex II); and it is referred to in the WAEMU treaty in terms of the need for national fiscal policies to be consistent with the common monetary policy.

Table 58. Banking Supervision in the Two Unions of the CFA Franc Zone

	West African Economic and Monetary Union		Central African Economic and Monetary Community	
	Content	Implementation, comments	Content	Implementation, comments
Regulatory framework	Banking Commission, responsible for the supervision of banks, credit institutions, and other specialized financial institutions, including granting or withdrawing banking licenses, and enforcing banking regulations.	Established 1989, effective 1990. Supervision is ensured through banks' obligations to provide monthly financial accounts and through regular/exceptional inspections.	Central African Banking Committee (COBAC) responsible for the supervision of banks, credit institutions, and other specialized financial institutions, including granting or withdrawing banking licenses, and enforcing banking regulations.	Established 1990, effective 1992. Supervision is ensured through banks' obligations to provide monthly financial accounts and through regular/exceptional inspections.
Prudential ratios	• Solvency		• Solvency	
	—Capital ratio	Net capital/total credit (weighted) > 4 percent.	—Capital ratio	Net capital/total credit > 5 percent.
	—Quality of the banks' loan portfolios	Ratio of credit admissible to central bank refinancing to total credit fixed at 60 percent, effective January 1994.	—Coverage of fixed assets	Net capital and borrowings over 5 years/fixed assets of the bank > 100 percent.
	—Division of risk	Net capital/weighted categories of risk.	—Division of risk	Net capital/weighted categories of risk.
	• Liquidity		• Liquidity	
	—Liquidity ratio	Ratio of liquid assets (including a weighted amount of credit admissible to central bank refinancing) to short-term liabilities > 60 percent.	—Liquidity ratio	Ratio of liquid assets (including credit admissible to central bank refinancing) to short-term liabilities > 100 percent.
	—Risk of transformation	Ratio of medium and long-term resources to medium- and long-term assets > 75 percent.	—Risk of transformation	Ratio of medium- and long-term resources to medium- and long-term assets > 50 percent.

therefore a matter for consideration whether in due course this should not be the only control variable constituting a policy criterion at the level of the national agencies of the central bank—as long as there are understandings with the two central banks on the desirable level for the regional net domestic assets.

Banking Supervision

The economic crisis that beset most economies of the zone from the mid-1980s had serious consequences for the national banking systems of the unions, and led eventually to large-scale restructuring operations during 1989–92. To forestall the reemergence of such banking crises, and prevent financial and political interference at the national level, the Ministers of Finance of the unions established in 1990 two regional supervisory authorities—the WAEMU's Banking Commission and the COBAC (Commission Bancaire de l'Afrique Centrale), each chaired by the Governor of the respective regional central bank—to ensure independent and rigorous bank supervision at the regional level. New banking legislation was also issued in each of the member countries, and the banking commissions began operations in 1990 in the WAEMU and in 1992 in the CAEMC.

The mandate of the commissions is to protect depositors' interests and to assure the stability of the regions' banking systems. They are responsible in particular for (a) granting banking licenses; (b) appointing trustees and liquidators; (c) defining, and adapting as needed, prudential regulations; and (d) pronouncing injunctions and taking sanctions (including through the withdrawal of banking licenses). The scope of supervision includes all banking and other financial institutions.

The banking commissions discharge their responsibilities through (a) enforcement of the requirement for member banks to provide key accounts and statements of position on a monthly basis; and (b) periodic and detailed inspections of all banks of the unions, complemented, if needed, by ad hoc inspections on specific issues (for instance, prior to initiation of a sanction procedure). In the context of the monthly supervision, the commissions focus on three groups of prudential ratios, measuring respectively the banks' solvency, their liquidity, and the risks incurred in the transformation of short-term liabilities into long-term lending operations (Table 58).

The commissions publish annual surveillance reports on the banking systems. In the WAEMU, the soundness of the banking systems has strengthened markedly since the restructuring was completed. In the CAEMC, the new common regulatory and prudential standards are being enforced gradually. Union-wide, liquidity and solvency ratios have improved somewhat, in part because of the recovery of money demand in the aftermath of the devaluation, and in part because of improved business conditions (e.g., in the Central African Republic, Chad, and Gabon).

Annex IV Fund Technical Assistance to CFA Franc Countries

The table on the following pages provides details of technical assistance provided by the International Monetary Fund to the member countries of the CFA franc zone during the period 1989–95, in terms of both long-term expert assistance and mission assignments. The information in the table is categorized under the three Fund departments that provided the assistance: the Monetary and Exchange Affairs Department (MAE), formerly the Central Banking Department (CBD); the Fiscal Affairs Department (FAD); and the Statistics Department (STA).

Table 59. Fund Technical Assistance to CFA Franc Countries, 1989–95: Long-Term Expert (LTE) and Mission Assignments (M)

	MAE		FAD		STA	
Country	Task	Date	Task	Date	Task	Date
WAEMU						
Benin	BCEAO-Monetary Policy (LTE)	1/92–95	Introd. of budget nomenclature (M)	11/20/90–12/18/90		
			Advice on budget reform (M)	10/18–23/92		
			Inspection of expert assign. (M)	10/23/92		
			Tax administration (LTE)	9/91–9/94		
			Tax admin. follow-up (M)	3/5–3/15/95		
			Budget Accounting (LTE)	1/23/91–12/23/92		
Burkina Faso			VAT implementation (M)	10/7–17/91	Real sector/Gen. Economy (M)	1/90
			Budget classification (M)	11/11–11/22/91	Multisector (M)	7–8/95
			Part. IBRD Public Exp. Review (M)	6/7–24/92		
			VAT administration (M)	11/25/92–12/12/92		
			Budget General (M)	7/15–24/93		
			Budget General (LTE)	5/16/94–5/15/95		
			Tax administration (LTE)	5/19/93–5/18/94		
			Tax policy, Admin. and Customs (M)	6/12–24/95		
			Tax administration (M)	6/8–20/92		
			Consol. Budgetary Expend (M)	6/25/90–7/7/90		
Côte d'Ivoire	BCEAO—Bank Supervision (M)	1989–94	Budget & Treasury Consol. (M)	10/10–26/90	National Accounts (M)	6/95
			Review of Tax admin. (M)	9/26/91–10/9/91		
	Inspection of CBD experts (M)	10/92	Tax Policy (M)	11/29/93–12/5/93		
	Bank Supervision (LTE)	9/91–92	Tax Admin. & Policy (M)	9/14/90–10/3/90		
	BCEAO-Bank Restructuring (M)	5/93 & 1/94	Public expenditure management (M)	11/28/94–12/2/94		
			Tax Policy, Admin. & Customs (M)	5/24/95–6/12/95		
			Tax Policy, Admin. & Customs (M)	5/26/95–6/12/95		
Mali	Inspection CBD experts (M)	12/89	Technical Inspection Visit (M)	11/19–22/90	BOP statistics (M)	10/90–11/90
	External Debt (M)	6/90–8/90	Tax administration (M)	11/9/92–12/2/92	Multitopic (M)	7/91
			Tax admin. assessment (M)	4/8–13/95	BOP statistics (M)	5/93
			Seminar-taxation on gov't procurement (M)	6/12–14/95	Natl. Acc. (LTE)	5/96–3/96
Niger	External debt data management (LTE)	7/90–1/93	Discuss revenue situation (M)	9/10–21/90	BOP statistics (M)	1–2/92
			Tax Policy & Administration (M)	11/20–12/10/93	Government finance statistics (M)	4–5/94
					National Accounts (M)	7/95

Senegal	BCEAO—Monetary & Operation (M)	10–11/89	BCEAO/COFEB Public Fin. Course (M)	5/6–18/90	Seminar on Money and Banking (M)	4/90
	Inspection of CBD experts (M)	12/89	Seminar on tax and budget issues (M)	1/14–18/91	Cooperation visit w/BCEAO (M)	7/91
	Financial sector reform (M)	6/92	BCEAO/COFEB Public Finance Seminar (M)	5/7–20/91	BOP (M)	7/92
			BCEAO Training (M)	5/11–24/95	BCEAO seminar on Government Finance (M)	1/93
			COFEB Seminar (M)	5/16–29/93	BOP Seminar (M)	2–3/94
			Tax Admin. w/WAMU (M)	12/12–18/93	Money & Banking Seminar (M)	3–4/95
			BCEAO Seminar (M)	5/15–21/94		
			Social Safety Net (M)	11/28–12/16/94		
			COFEB Seminar (M)	5/22–6/2/95		
			Customs administration (LTE)	10/91–1/94		
Togo	Issuance of Treasury bills (M)	12/90	Tax and tariff reform implem. (M)	11/22–12/4/91		
			Budget and accounting reform (M)	5/2–23/91		
			Tax assessment (M)	2/17–3/6/92		
			Tax and follow-up customs (M)	11/23–12/17/91		
			UMOA Study (M)	12/8–16/93		
			Short-term Country Resident Expert Assignment (M)	1/31/94–2/18/94		
			Budget General (LTE)	9/94–9/95		
			Tax Administration (LTE)	2/95–2/96		
			Installation of Tax Advisor (M)	3/15–18/95		
			Tax Administration (LTE)	8/15/92–2/23/93		
BCEAO	Bank Supervision & Regulation (LTE)	9/89–90				
	Part. in WB BCEAO seminar (M)	5/91				
CAEMC						
Cameroon	Monetary Instrument (M)	9/90	Non-oil tax revenue budget (M)	11/3–11/20/90	National Accounts (M)	10/90
	BEAC—Foreign Exchange (M)	9/90	Budget policy follow-up (M)	5/13–5/24/91	Review/follow-up data resources (M)	4/91
	BEAC—Bank Supervision (M)	1991–94	Follow-up budgetary policy (M)	4/23–5/4/92	Money and Banking (M)	11/92
	BEAC—Bank Restructuring (M)	6/93	CAECU Tax reform (M)	10/21–11/01/92	Government Finance (M)	7/93
	BEAC—Monetary Policy Workshop (M)	2/94	Tax Policy and Administration (M)	8/28–9/4/93		
			Tax Administration (M)	1/20–2/6/94	Balance of Payments (M)	5/95
	BEAC—Monetary Policy Review (M)	7/94	CAECU Seminar (M)	6/13–6/19/94		
Central African Republic			Customs Administration (M)	7/8–13/91		
			CAECU Tax Reform (M)	10/17–21/92		
			Tax Administration (M)	2/1–17/93		
			Tax & Customs Administration (M)	6/20–30/94		

Table 59 *(concluded)*

	MAE		FAD		STA	
Country	Task	Date	Task	Date	Task	Date
Chad			Tax Administration (M)	9/4–20/90		
			Follow-up on taxation (M)	7/6–13/91		
			Tax Administration (M)	12/2–17/91		
			CAECU Tax Reform (M)	10/15–17/92		
			Customs Administration (LTE)	10/94–10/95		
			Customs Administration (M)	8/30–9/10/94		
			Customs Administration/Follow-Up (M)	5/20–25/95		
Congo			CAECU Tax Reform (M)	10/15–19/92		
			CAECU meeting (M)	12/7/92		
			Tax & Customs Administration (M)	10/28–11/15/94		
Equatorial Guinea			CAECU Tax Reform (M)	10/25–30/92		
			Tax Administration Inspection (M)	1/10–16/93		
			Follow-up meetings to CAECU (M)	12/9–11/92		
			Tax Administration (LTE)	7/92–2/94		
			Mtg. on CAECU Customs Tariff (M)	4/6–7/95		
			Multipurpose mission (M)	2/18–27/93		
Gabon			Workshop of CAECU Regulatory Reform (M)	11/4–9/91	BEAC Seminar on Money & Banking (M)	3/90
			CAECU Tax Reform (M)	10/20–24/92	Balance of Payments Seminar (M)	7/94
			Tax Administration (M)	10/9–23/93		
			Tax Administration Follow-up (M)	2/6–8/94		
			Balance sheet revaluation seminar (M)	1/19–26/95		
			Budget preparation and control (M)	4/11–22/95		
BEAC	Bank Supervision and Regulation (LT Experts)	1989 & 1990				
Comoros	Bank Supervision and Regulation (M)	1989–93	Tariff reform (M)	7/21–27/91		
			Tax & Customs Administration (M)	3/15–26/93		
			Customs Administration (M)	5/10–17/93		
			Tax & Customs Administration (M)	8/23–10/23/93		

Annex V World Bank Group Technical Assistance to CFA Franc Countries

Since fiscal year 1990, the World Bank Group has provided support for improving economic management under the following technical assistance operations (to September 1995).

Benin

The fiscal year 1995 Economic Management Project (US$6.0 million equivalent) focuses on investment programming, budgeting, national accounts and procurement policies. In the context of the project, the Ministry of Planning will be reorganized around the main missions of economic analysis, public investment programming and monitoring, and supervision of the remaining public enterprises. The project will include an action plan to restructure the debt agency and the statistical office. All the budgeting procedures will be reviewed; the relationship between the Ministries of Plan and Finance, and the spending ministries will be reviewed with the purpose of ensuring better budgetary preparation procedures.

Burkina Faso

The fiscal year 1992 Public Institutional Development Project (US$15 million equivalent) provides support for capacity-building in budgetary management, civil service reform, statistical information, and business law reform. The fiscal year 1993 Private Sector Assistance Project (US$7 million) focuses on institutional support for banking, public enterprise, and private sector reforms.

Côte d'Ivoire

The fiscal year 1992 Privatization Support Project (US$15 million equivalent) provides critical institutional and technical support to the government's privatization program, which is a key component of Côte d'Ivoire's medium-term macroeconomic adjustment program. The project also provides assistance to acquaint the authorities with up-to-date debt reduction and restructuring options. The fiscal year 1993 Economic Management Project (US$17 million equivalent) provides support for improving macroeconomic management, including parapublic enterprise reform, a revamping of the statistical apparatus, civil service reform, and legal and judiciary reform. The fiscal year 1993 Human Resources Development Management Project (US$6.7 million equivalent) is designed to increase the capacity of social sector ministries that account for a large share in government recurrent expenditure, to better prepare and execute their budgets, and to better manage the related human resources. The fiscal year 1994 National Agricultural Services Support Project (US$21.8 million equivalent) provides help for restructuring government agricultural services and increasing farmers' participation in the policy making process. The fiscal year 1994 Labor Force Training Support Project (US$17 million equivalent) aims at improving the employability and productivity of some categories of workers through skill training.

Mali

The fiscal year 1991 Structural Adjustment Loan I (US$70 million equivalent) has a technical assistance component that aims at strengthening the institutional capacity to implement the economic reform agenda. The government requested and has been granted permission to use the remaining funds of this component for the construction of customs posts in border areas.

Niger

The Public Institutional Development Project (under preparation, about US$10 million equivalent) aims at strengthening economic management (budgetary process, resource mobilization), civil service reform, and the legal/regulatory framework for business activities.

Senegal

The fiscal year 1988 Development Management Project (US$17 million equivalent) supports institutions responsible for macroeconomic management and the civil service. Key activities include consolidating public investment programming, strengthening debt management and statistical systems, and improving civil service efficiency through organizational audits of selected ministries.

Togo

A public expenditure review will commence shortly to analyze the structure of public expenditure and present recommendations to restructure its composition. To strengthen public management in the areas of planning, programming, and budgeting, an Institutional Assessment Study will be undertaken in 1996. The study will review the government's organizational structure, assess the development needs of key ministries and support the government's decentralization objectives.

Cameroon

The fiscal year 1990 Economic Management Project (US$9 million equivalent) aimed at improving the government's macroeconomic management, public investment programming, debt servicing, and statistical information as well as restructuring the civil service, key government agencies, and the public enterprise sector.

Central African Republic

The fiscal year 1995 Economic Management Project (US$13.2 million equivalent) provides assistance in (i) public investment programming and monitoring; (ii) reform of management of the civil service; (iii) revenue collection and spending control improvement; and (iv) public enterprise reform.

Chad

The fiscal year 1988 Economic and Financial Management Project (US$12.8 million equivalent) aims at strengthening government institutions and coordination mechanisms. After its recent restructuring, the project focuses on revenue enhancement (including for customs duties and petroleum taxes), strengthening expenditure control and treasury management, and support for the formulation of medium-term reform programs.

Congo

In FY 1994, the World Bank declared the Congo IDA eligible and supported a first-phase economic recovery program through a US$100 million Economic Recovery Credit (ERC). The ERC aimed at curtailing public expenditure and implementing key structural measures to prepare the ground for a deeper transformation of the economy and reduction in the public sector. The second phase of the economic recovery program will be supported by a privatization and capacity building project that is tentatively scheduled to be submitted to the Board in July 1995. The project aims at accelerating divestiture of public enterprises, introducing a competitive environment in the utility and petroleum sectors, and facilitating private sector development. Specifically, the project will provide support to the government in: (i) preparing regulatory frameworks for the five major public enterprises in control of petroleum distribution, transportation, telecommunications, power and water distribution and opening up the sectors to competition progressively; (ii) conducting the privatization of these major public enterprises; (iii) liquidating other nonviable PEs; and (iv) supporting regulation and competition in the financial sector and reforms in banking institutions.

Gabon

The fiscal year 1990 Economic Management Project (US$5 million equivalent), recently concluded, provided support to the government's structural adjustment program by strengthening the ministries in key areas of economic management. Civil service reform and small- and medium-scale enterprise development were the core elements. Following the adjustment of the parity of the CFA franc on January 12, 1994, a quick-disbursing economic recovery loan (US$30 million equivalent) to support the immediate accompanying measures that are part of the adjustment program was approved by the Board on June 21, 1994, and has been fully disbursed. In addition, a transport sector technical assistance loan (US$5.2 million equivalent) was approved on July 7, 1994. A public expenditure review (PER) with a view of helping the government formulate a high-return and sustainable program of public expenditure that supports its development objectives was conducted by the World Bank in April 1995.

Comoros

The current and ongoing assistance provided under the MERCAP involves strengthening the economic management capacity of the government through capacity building and on-the-job training in the Ministry of Finance and the Planning Directorate, which has included: (1) budget preparation and the monitoring of its execution with a computerized system; (2) preparation and monitoring of the rolling three-year public investment program; and (3) technical support and training in the areas of debt and treasury accounts management, national accounts compilation, and macroeconomic analysis and forecasting.

References

AFRISTAT, "Traité d'Harmonisation des Statitistiques Africaines," Abidjan (September 21, 1993).

Baldet, J., F.L. Corfmat, and J.P. Cornély, "Current Tax Issues in CFA Countries," Fiscal Affairs Department, IMF, 1990.

Banque Centrale des Etats de l'Afrique de l'Ouest, *Rapports Annuels.*

———, "Situation Economique, Financière, et Monétaire des Etats de l'UEMOA en 1994," BCEAO (March 1995).

———, "Rapport du Gouverneur sur la Situation Economique, Financière, et Monétaire des Etats de l'UEMOA un an après le changement de parité du franc CFA" BCEAO (March 17, 1995).

Banque des Etats de l'Afrique Centrale, *Rapports Annuels.*

———, "Propositions pour une Relance de l'Integration Economique et Sociale en UDEAC," *Report of the Regional Committee of Experts*, BEAC (1993).

Berg, Elliot, "Intégration Economique en Afrique de l'Ouest, Problèmes et Stratégie," *Revue d'Economie du Développement* (February 1993), pp. 51–82.

Boughton, James, "The CFA Franc Zone: Currency Union and Monetary Standard," IMF Working Paper 91/133 (1991).

Caisse Française de Développement, "Rapport de Synthèse sur la Relance des Economies de la Zone Franc," C.F.D. Paris (November 1994).

Clément, Jean A.P., "Franc Zone: Realignment Is Vital Element of New Strategy," *IMF Survey Special Supplement* (March 21, 1994), pp. 1–3.

———, "Macroeconomic Stability and Structural Reforms Are Key to Effective Management," *IMF Survey Special Supplement* (March 21, 1994), pp. 11–12.

———, "Questions and Answers: Defining the Issues and Assessing Prospects," *IMF Survey Special Supplement* (March 21, 1994), pp. 4–6.

———, "Rationale for the CFA Franc Realignment," *IMF Survey*, Vol. 23 (February 7, 1994), pp. 33–36.

———, "Striving for Stability: CFA Franc Realignment," IMF and World Bank, *Finance and Development* (June 1994), pp. 10–13.

———, "Aftermath of the CFA Franc Devaluation," IMF and World Bank, *Finance and Development* (June 1995), pp. 24–27.

Conférence Interafricaine des Marchés d'Assurances (CIMA), "Traité Instituant une Organisation Intégrée de l'Industrie des Assurances dans les Etats Africains," Yaoundé (July 10, 1992).

———, "Code des Assurances des Etats Membres de la CIMA," Yaoundé (July 10, 1992).

Conférence Interafricaine de la Prévoyance Sociale, "Traité Instituant une Conférence Interafricaine de la Prévoyance Sociale," Abidjan (September 21, 1993).

De Lafond, Tristan, "Le Traité Relatif à l'Harmonisation du Droit des Affaires en Afrique," *Gazette du Palais*, Paris (September 1985).

Dhonte, Pierre, "La Dévaluation du Franc CFA, Premiers Résultats," *Chroniques Economiques*, SEDIS, No. 8 (August 15, 1994), pp. 268–69.

Goreux, Louis M., "La Dévaluation du Franc CFA; Un Premier Bilan en Decembre 1995," World Bank (December 1995).

Guillaumont, Patrick et Sylvianne, "L'Intégration Economique un Nouvel Enjeu pour la Zone Franc," *Revue d'Economie du Développement* (February 1993), pp. 83–112.

———, "Zone Franc et Développement Africain," *Economica*, Ministère de la Coopération, Paris (1985).

———, "Stratégies de Développement Comparées. Zone Franc et Hors Zone Franc," *Economica,* Ministère de la Coopération, Paris (1988).

———, "La Zone Franc à un Tournant: Vers l'Intégration Régionale," in *La France et l'Afrique. Vade-Mecum pour un Nouveau Voyage,* ed. by S. Michaïlof (Paris: Kathala, 1993), pp. 411–22.

International Monetary Fund, "Issues in the Operations of Monetary Unions and Common Currency Areas," unpublished paper (May 23, 1991).

———, "A Review of the CFA Franc Arrangements," unpublished paper (July 9, 1990).

———, *World Economic Outlook* (May 1994), Box 6, pp. 60–61.

Julienne, Robert, "Vingt ans d'Institutions Monétaires Ouest Africaines, 1955–1975 (Paris: l'Harmatan, 1989).

Kouwenaar, Arend, "Price and Volume Effects of a Devaluation in Developing Countries," IMF Working Paper 91/130 (December 1991).

Ministère de la Coopération, "La Zone Franc Après la Dévaluation du Franc CFA," *Les Notes de la Coopération Française, Macroéconomie Finances*, Paris (July 1995).

Neurisse, André, "Le Franc CFA," Librairie de Droit et Jurisprudence, Paris (1987).

Nuven, Diep, "Linkage in Price Level and Inflation Rate Between CFA Franc Zone Countries and France," IMF Working Paper 94/93 (1993).

Organisation pour l'Harmonisation en Afrique du Droit des Affaires, "Traité relatif à l'harmonisation en Afrique du droit des affaires en Afrique," Port-Louis (October 19, 1993).

Touré, Mamadou, "New Strategy of Franc Zone Countries Aims to Stimulate Growth and Reduce Poverty," *IMF Survey, Special Supplement* (March 21, 1994), pp. 7–10.

Union Economique et Monétaire Ouest Africaine, "Traité de l'Union Economique et Monétaire Ouest Africaine," Dakar (January 10, 1994).

———, Protocole additionnel n° 1 relatif aux organes de Contrôle de l'Union Economique et Monétaire Ouest Africaine (UEMOA), Dakar (January 10, 1994).

———, Protocole additional n° 11 relatif aux Politiques Sectorielles de l'Union Economique et Monétaire Ouest Africaine (UEMOA), Dakar (January 10, 1994).

Vinay, Bernard, "Zone Franc et Coopération Monétaire," Ministère de la Coopération et du Développement, Paris, 2ème édition, (1988).

Recent Occasional Papers of the International Monetary Fund

138. Aftermath of the CFA Franc Devaluation, by Jean A.P. Clément, with Johannes Mueller, Stéphane Cossé, and Jean Le Dem. 1996

137. The Lao People's Democratic Republic: Systemic Transformation and Adjustment, edited by Ichiro Otani and Chi Do Pham. 1996.

136. Jordan: Strategy for Adjustment and Growth, edited by Edouard Maciejewski and Ahsan Mansur. 1996.

135. Vietnam: Transition to a Market Economy, by John R. Dodsworth, Erich Spitäller, Michael Braulke, Keon Hyok Lee, Kenneth Miranda, Christian Mulder, Hisanobu Shishido, and Krishna Srinivasan. 1996.

134. India: Economic Reform and Growth, by Ajai Chopra, Charles Collyns, Richard Hemming, and Karen Parker with Woosik Chu and Oliver Fratzscher. 1995.

133. Policy Experiences and Issues in the Baltics, Russia, and Other Countries of the Former Soviet Union, edited by Daniel A. Citrin and Ashok K. Lahiri. 1995.

132. Financial Fragilities in Latin America: The 1980s and 1990s, by Liliana Rojas-Suárez and Steven R. Weisbrod. 1995.

131. Capital Account Convertibility: Review of Experience and Implications for IMF Policies, by staff teams headed by Peter J. Quirk and Owen Evans. 1995.

130. Challenges to the Swedish Welfare State, by Desmond Lachman, Adam Bennett, John H. Green, Robert Hagemann, and Ramana Ramaswamy. 1995.

129. IMF Conditionality: Experience Under Stand-By and Extended Arrangements. Part II: Background Papers. Susan Schadler, Editor, with Adam Bennett, Maria Carkovic, Louis Dicks-Mireaux, Mauro Mecagni, James H.J. Morsink, and Miguel A. Savastano. 1995.

128. IMF Conditionality: Experience Under Stand-By and Extended Arrangements. Part I: Key Issues and Findings, by Susan Schadler, Adam Bennett, Maria Carkovic, Louis Dicks-Mireaux, Mauro Mecagni, James H.J. Morsink, and Miguel A. Savastano. 1995.

127. Road Maps of the Transition: The Baltics, the Czech Republic, Hungary, and Russia, by Biswajit Banerjee, Vincent Koen, Thomas Krueger, Mark S. Lutz, Michael Marrese, and Tapio O. Saavalainen. 1995.

126. The Adoption of Indirect Instruments of Monetary Policy, by a Staff Team headed by William E. Alexander, Tomás J.T. Baliño, and Charles Enoch. 1995.

125. United Germany: The First Five Years—Performance and Policy Issues, by Robert Corker, Robert A. Feldman, Karl Habermeier, Hari Vittas, and Tessa van der Willigen. 1995.

124. Saving Behavior and the Asset Price "Bubble" in Japan: Analytical Studies, edited by Ulrich Baumgartner and Guy Meredith. 1995.

123. Comprehensive Tax Reform: The Colombian Experience, edited by Parthasarathi Shome. 1995.

122. Capital Flows in the APEC Region, edited by Mohsin S. Khan and Carmen M. Reinhart. 1995.

121. Uganda: Adjustment with Growth, 1987–94, by Robert L. Sharer, Hema R. De Zoysa, and Calvin A. McDonald. 1995.

120. Economic Dislocation and Recovery in Lebanon, by Sena Eken, Paul Cashin, S. Nuri Erbas, Jose Martelino, and Adnan Mazarei. 1995.

119. Singapore: A Case Study in Rapid Development, edited by Kenneth Bercuson with a staff team comprising Robert G. Carling, Aasim M. Husain, Thomas Rumbaugh, and Rachel van Elkan. 1995.

118. Sub-Saharan Africa: Growth, Savings, and Investment, by Michael T. Hadjimichael, Dhaneshwar Ghura, Martin Mühleisen, Roger Nord, and E. Murat Uçer. 1995.

117. Resilience and Growth Through Sustained Adjustment: The Moroccan Experience, by Saleh M. Nsouli, Sena Eken, Klaus Enders, Van-Can Thai, Jörg Decressin, and Filippo Cartiglia, with Janet Bungay. 1995.

116. Improving the International Monetary System: Constraints and Possibilities, by Michael Mussa, Morris Goldstein, Peter B. Clark, Donald J. Mathieson, and Tamim Bayoumi. 1994.

115. Exchange Rates and Economic Fundamentals: A Framework for Analysis, by Peter B. Clark, Leonardo Bartolini, Tamim Bayoumi, and Steven Symansky. 1994.

114. Economic Reform in China: A New Phase, by Wanda Tseng, Hoe Ee Khor, Kalpana Kochhar, Dubravko Mihaljek, and David Burton. 1994.

113. Poland: The Path to a Market Economy, by Liam P. Ebrill, Ajai Chopra, Charalambos Christofides, Paul Mylonas, Inci Otker, and Gerd Schwartz. 1994.

112. The Behavior of Non-Oil Commodity Prices, by Eduardo Borensztein, Mohsin S. Khan, Carmen M. Reinhart, and Peter Wickham. 1994.

111. The Russian Federation in Transition: External Developments, by Benedicte Vibe Christensen. 1994.

110. Limiting Central Bank Credit to the Government: Theory and Practice, by Carlo Cottarelli. 1993.

109. The Path to Convertibility and Growth: The Tunisian Experience, by Saleh M. Nsouli, Sena Eken, Paul Duran, Gerwin Bell, and Zühtü Yücelik. 1993.

108. Recent Experiences with Surges in Capital Inflows, by Susan Schadler, Maria Carkovic, Adam Bennett, and Robert Kahn. 1993.

107. China at the Threshold of a Market Economy, by Michael W. Bell, Hoe Ee Khor, and Kalpana Kochhar with Jun Ma, Simon N'guiamba, and Rajiv Lall. 1993.

106. Economic Adjustment in Low-Income Countries: Experience Under the Enhanced Structural Adjustment Facility, by Susan Schadler, Franek Rozwadowski, Siddharth Tiwari, and David O. Robinson. 1993.

105. The Structure and Operation of the World Gold Market, by Gary O'Callaghan. 1993.

104. Price Liberalization in Russia: Behavior of Prices, Household Incomes, and Consumption During the First Year, by Vincent Koen and Steven Phillips. 1993.

103. Liberalization of the Capital Account: Experiences and Issues, by Donald J. Mathieson and Liliana Rojas-Suárez. 1993.

102. Financial Sector Reforms and Exchange Arrangements in Eastern Europe. Part I: Financial Markets and Intermediation, by Guillermo A. Calvo and Manmohan S. Kumar. Part II: Exchange Arrangements of Previously Centrally Planned Economies, by Eduardo Borensztein and Paul R. Masson. 1993.

101. Spain: Converging with the European Community, by Michel Galy, Gonzalo Pastor, and Thierry Pujol. 1993.

100. The Gambia: Economic Adjustment in a Small Open Economy, by Michael T. Hadjimichael, Thomas Rumbaugh, and Eric Verreydt. 1992.

99. Mexico: The Strategy to Achieve Sustained Economic Growth, edited by Claudio Loser and Eliot Kalter. 1992.

98. Albania: From Isolation Toward Reform, by Mario I. Blejer, Mauro Mecagni, Ratna Sahay, Richard Hides, Barry Johnston, Piroska Nagy, and Roy Pepper. 1992.

97. Rules and Discretion in International Economic Policy, by Manuel Guitián. 1992.

96. Policy Issues in the Evolving International Monetary System, by Morris Goldstein, Peter Isard, Paul R. Masson, and Mark P. Taylor. 1992.

95. The Fiscal Dimensions of Adjustment in Low-Income Countries, by Karim Nashashibi, Sanjeev Gupta, Claire Liuksila, Henri Lorie, and Walter Mahler. 1992. 94. Tax Harmonization in the European Community: Policy Issues and Analysis, edited by George Kopits. 1992.

94. Tax Harmonization in the European Community: Policy Issues and Analysis, edited by George Kopits. 1992.

Note: For information on the title and availability of Occasional Papers not listed, please consult the IMF Publications Catalog or contact IMF Publication Services.